# Real Food
### *for*
# *Diabetics*

Molly Perham

# Real Food
*for*
# *Diabetics*

Molly Perham

## foulsham
LONDON • NEW YORK • TORONTO • SYDNEY

# foulsham

The Publishing House, Bennets Close, Cippenham,
Slough, Berkshire, SL1 5AP, England

ISBN 0-572-02728-1

Copyright © 2001 Molly Perham

Cover photograph by Peter Howard Smith

The publication of this book does not constitute
the practice of medicine, and this book does not
attempt to replace any diet or instructions from
your doctor. The author and publisher advise the
reader to check with a doctor before
administering any medication or undertaking any
course of treatment or exercise.

Printed in Great Britain by Cox & Wyman Ltd, Reading, Berkshire

# Contents

# Introduction

*I*f you have bought this book, or been given it, then you or a member of your family has probably been diagnosed with diabetes. You may be completely new to the condition and anxious to learn what someone with diabetes should be eating; or diabetes may be well-known to you – perhaps it runs in your family – and you are looking for new ideas to brighten up your meals. Whichever of these situations applies to you, the message is the same: there is no need to stick to a special 'diabetic' diet. All you need to do is aim for a healthy, balanced diet of the kind that is suitable for everyone – so the recipes in this book can be enjoyed by every member of the family, not just those who have diabetes.

This book has been written to help you to live a healthy and normal life without the worry and inconvenience of inventing and preparing special meals. A healthy lifestyle, including a healthy, balanced diet, exercise and medication, if appropriate, can mean that you can continue your normal, everyday activities – so read on, and learn how to manage your condition and enjoy eating!

# Living with diabetes

If you have diabetes, your body does not produce sufficient insulin to control the amount of glucose (sugar) in your blood. Normally, when we eat any starchy or sugary foods (carbohydrate), such as a biscuit or slice of bread, it enters the stomach and then the intestine, where it is digested or broken down into glucose. Glucose then passes into the bloodstream. Without enough insulin, excessive glucose remains in the bloodstream.

People with diabetes fall into two groups: those who are insulin-dependent, also known as Type 1, and those who are non-insulin-dependent, or Type 2.

People with Type 1, insulin-dependent, diabetes make no insulin at all because most or all of the cells that produce it have been destroyed. This type of diabetes usually appears in children and adults under 40, and there is some tendency for it to run in families. It may be triggered by a viral infection or by an abnormal reaction against the insulin-producing cells.

Type 2, non-insulin-dependent, diabetes is the more common type of diabetes. The body either cannot produce enough insulin or the insulin that is produced is not properly used by the body. This type of diabetes usually affects people over 40, those who have a genetic predisposition to diabetes; being overweight is a contributory cause to Type 2 diabetes. This type currently affects about 2 per cent of the UK population, and is on the increase.

## Controlling diabetes

In order to treat diabetes, the blood-sugar levels must be artificially controlled. In the case of Type 1 diabetes, this is done by administering insulin injections and eating a healthy, balanced diet. Type 2 diabetes may be treated by diet alone, or by diet and tablets, or occasionally by diet and insulin injections. Diet is therefore fundamental to the management of both types of diabetes, and following a healthy eating regime, with exercise and medication, if necessary, will help to keep blood-sugar levels stable. It is also important to eat your meals at regular intervals throughout the day (people on insulin in particular should always have a mid-morning and mid-afternoon snack).

Controlling your blood-sugar levels is vital because poorly controlled diabetes is more likely to lead to diabetic complications such as damage to the eyes, kidneys, nerves, heart and major arteries. It is also important to take regular exercise and watch your weight.

# A healthy diet

So what is this healthy diet? The diet for diabetes is the same healthy eating diet suitable for all. Everyone, whether they have diabetes or not, should eat at least five portions of fruit and vegetables each day and plenty of high-starch, high-fibre foods. We should all also try to cut down on fat and sugar and watch our intake of salt. However, this advice is all the more important for people with diabetes, who are predisposed to heart disease, strokes and high blood pressure. Always bear in mind the following when planning meals:

◇ Cut down on the animal (saturated) fat in meat recipes by buying lean meat and cut off any extra fat. Cut the skin off chicken and turkey.

◇ Choose low-fat dairy products wherever possible. The recipes in this book use polyunsaturated oils for cooking, and sunflower margarine or low-fat spread instead of butter (check the labels and choose brands that are suitable for cooking as well as spreading).

◇ Use skimmed or semi-skimmed milk, not full-cream.

◇ Cut down on cheese and use reduced-fat or low-fat varieties.

◇ Cut down on added sugar. Wherever possible, choose low-sugar products – there is a huge range now available in supermarkets. Desserts can be sweetened naturally with fruit or fruit juice.

◇ Use only a small amount of salt when cooking. I have used herbs and spices extensively in the recipes in this book as they improve the flavour of the dishes and reduce the amount of salt needed.

◇ When buying canned beans and vegetables, look for those labelled 'no added salt or sugar'.

◇ Watch your weight – ask your dietitian for individual advice.

## food choices

Healthy foods are those that are low in fat and sugar, and high in fibre. Starchy (carbohydrate) foods, such as chapatis, yams, potatoes, rice, pasta, bread and cereals, should form the basis of each meal: they are digested and released into the blood at a slow, steady rate, thus helping to control blood-sugar levels. Different carbohydrate foods have dramatically different effects on blood-sugar levels, so, in order to keep your blood-sugar level stable, you should eat a wide variety of starchy foods, including high-fibre varities.

The important thing to remember when planning your diet is balance. No foods are completely forbidden, but some will form a regular part of your diet, while others can be occasional treats.

Here are some healthy options:

◇ Fresh fruit and vegetables

◇ Lean meat, poultry and fish

◇ Low-fat milk, cheese and yoghurt

◇ Pulses – peas, beans and lentils

◇ Pasta, preferably wholemeal

◇ Rice (particularly basmati and brown) and other grains

◇ Oats

◇ Wholemeal bread and flour

◇ High-fibre, unsweetened breakfast cereals such as Branflakes and All-Bran

If you are given chocolate or sweets – or a child with diabetes is given a chocolate Easter egg or similar gift – it is best to spread it out and not eat it all in one go.

If you like your tea and coffee sweet, use artificial sweetener instead of sugar. In time, you will probably find that your taste for sweet things diminishes as you get used to your healthy diet.

In general, remember that you are aiming for a healthy, balanced diet.

## Your storecupboard for healthy eating

*f*or the recipes in this book – and for general day-to-day catering – I recommend that you keep the following items in your storecupboard, fridge or freezer.

### Dry stores and packets

◇ Flour – self-raising (self-rising), plain (all-purpose), wholemeal
◇ Cornflour (cornstarch)
◇ Sugar and/or artificial sweetener
◇ Oats – rolled porridge oats, oatflakes and oatmeal
◇ Egg noodles
◇ Pasta – spaghetti, lasagne, tagliatelle, any pasta shapes and soup pasta
◇ Polenta
◇ Rice – basmati and brown
◇ Bulghar (cracked wheat)
◇ Couscous
◇ Pot barley
◇ Lentils – red and green
◇ Nuts – brazils, cashews, unsalted peanuts, walnuts, pine nuts and flaked (slivered) almonds
◇ Seeds – sesame and sunflower
◇ Dried fruit – raisins, apricots and mixed
◇ Sugar-free jelly (jello) crystals

### Cans, jars and bottles

◇ Fish – tuna, salmon and sardines
◇ Sweetcorn (corn)
◇ Chick peas (garbanzos)
◇ Beans – butter (lima), borlotti, cannellini, flageolet, red kidney
◇ Tomatoes
◇ Tomato purée (paste)

◇ Sun-dried tomatoes
◇ Pesto
◇ Polyunsaturated oils – olive, sunflower, vegetable, sesame
◇ Olives
◇ Low-fat mayonnaise
◇ Clear honey

# Herbs and flavourings

◇ Salt
◇ Wine vinegar
◇ Lemon juice
◇ Mustard – English and Dijon
◇ Sauces – Worcestershire, Tabasco, soy, chilli
◇ Stock cubes – vegetable, chicken and beef
◇ Spices – ground cinnamon, ginger, chilli powder, cumin, coriander, paprika and turmeric; grated nutmeg; whole black peppercorns, cinnamon sticks, cloves, cardamom pods and cumin seeds
◇ Dried herbs – basil, bay leaves, sage, thyme and mixed herbs
◇ Fresh herbs – basil, chives, coriander (cilantro), oregano, mint, parsley, rosemary, sage and thyme
◇ Root ginger (fresh, or ready-crushed in jars)
◇ Garlic, fresh cloves and dried granules

# Chilled and frozen

◇ Milk – skimmed or semi-skimmed
◇ Apple juice – unsweetened, concentrated
◇ Sunflower margarine or low-fat spread
◇ Plain low-fat yoghurt
◇ Low-fat crème fraîche
◇ Low-fat cottage cheese and cream cheese
◇ Reduced-fat Cheddar cheese
◇ Parmesan cheese
◇ Eggs
◇ Frozen vegetables – peas, sweetcorn (corn) and spinach

# Notes on the recipes

◇ Do not mix metric, imperial or American measures. Follow one set only.

◇ All spoon measures are level: 1 tsp = 5 ml; 1 tbsp = 15 ml.

◇ American terms are given in brackets.

◇ Eggs are medium unless otherwise stated.

◇ Always wash, peel, core and seed, if necessary, fresh foods before use. Ensure that all produce is as fresh as possible and in good condition.

◇ Seasoning and the use of strongly flavoured ingredients, such as onions and garlic, are very much a matter of personal taste. Taste the food as you cook and adjust the quantity of seasonings to suit your own preference.

◇ Always use fresh herbs unless dried are specifically called for. If it is necessary to use dried herbs, use half the quantity stated. Chopped, frozen varieties are much better than dried. There is no substitute for fresh parsley or coriander (cilantro).

◇ Can sizes are approximate and will depend on the particular brand.

# Breakfast, morning coffee and afternoon tea

*B*reakfast is the most important meal of the day for anyone, but particularly if you have diabetes. A bowl of cereal followed by toast and marmalade is fine for breakfast – but choose a high-fibre breakfast cereal, such as Branflakes, All-Bran, muesli or porridge, rather than Cornflakes or Rice Crispies, and use skimmed or semi-skimmed milk to reduce your intake of fat. Eat wholemeal and multi-grain bread instead of white, and use a low-fat spread instead of butter. Supermarkets now stock a good range of reduced-sugar marmalades and jams (conserves), although these do not keep as long as ordinary varieties. Add fresh or dried fruit to your breakfast menu whenever you can, to increase your intake of fibre and provide valuable vitamins and minerals.

The recipes in this section are perfect for breakfast, but many of them are also ideal as a snack with your mid-morning coffee, or afternoon cup of tea.

# Quick muesli
SERVES 1

*When you buy ready-packaged muesli, check the list of ingredients to see how much sugar there is in it. This recipe for home-made muesli uses no sugar at all – the raisins provide all the sweetness it needs.*

45 ml/3 tbsp porridge oats or oatflakes
15 ml/1 tbsp wheat or bran flakes
25 g/1 oz/3 tbsp raisins
25 g/1 oz/¼ cup chopped mixed nuts
150 ml/¼ pt/⅔ cup skimmed or semi-skimmed milk

① Mix together all the ingredients and pour over the milk.

PREPARATION TIME: 2 MINUTES

# Apple muesli
SERVES 1

*This is how muesli used to be prepared before it appeared on the supermarket shelves in packets. It's absolutely delicious, and doesn't require much more effort than opening a packet.*

30 ml/2 tbsp porridge oats or oatflakes
5 ml/1 tsp sesame seeds
25 g/1 oz/3 tbsp raisins
60 ml/4 tbsp water
1 small eating (dessert) apple
10 ml/2 tsp lemon juice
15–30 ml/2–3 tbsp plain low-fat yoghurt

① Put the oats, sesame seeds, raisins and water into a cereal bowl. Cover and leave overnight.

② When you are ready to eat, grate the apple on to the oats and sprinkle with the lemon juice. Spoon over the yoghurt and stir well to mix.

PREPARATION TIME: 3 MINUTES PLUS SOAKING

# Quick microwave porridge
### SERVES 1

*Oats are particularly good at helping to keep blood-sugar levels even, so porridge is an ideal breakfast. You can make it in a saucepan on top of the stove, or in a microwave – which is quicker and means that you don't have a saucepan to wash up.*

---

**30 ml/2 tbsp porridge oats**
**150 ml/¼ pt/⅔ cup skimmed or semi-skimmed milk**
**Salt, to taste**
**Artificial sweetener, to taste**
**25 g/1 oz/3 tbsp raisins (optional)**
**½ banana, sliced (optional)**

---

① Put the porridge oats and milk into a dish.

② Microwave for 2 minutes on High. If the porridge is too runny, give it a stir and microwave for another 30 seconds to 1 minute, but keep your eye on it in case it bubbles up and spills over the dish.

③ Add salt or artificial sweetener to taste, if preferred.

④ Eat the porridge plain, or add raisins and/or banana.

PREPARATION AND COOKING TIME: 3 MINUTES

# Scrambled eggs
### SERVES 1 OR 2

*Scrambled eggs make a quick and satisfying breakfast. Here is the basic version, plus a couple of variations on the next two pages.*

---

**2 eggs**
**15 ml/1 tbsp semi-skimmed milk**
**Salt and freshly ground black pepper**
**A knob of sunflower margarine or low-fat spread,**
**  plus extra for spreading**
**1–2 slices of wholemeal bread**

---

① Break the eggs into a bowl, add the milk and season with a pinch of salt and pepper. Beat well with a fork.

② Melt a knob of sunflower margarine or low-fat spread in a small, non-stick pan. Once it is foaming, remove from the heat, pour in the eggs and start stirring quickly. Return the pan to the heat and cook until just set, but still creamy. Do not overcook, or they will go rubbery.

③ Meanwhile, toast the bread, spread with sunflower margarine or low-fat spread and spoon the eggs on top.

PREPARATION AND COOKING TIME: 5 MINUTES

# Scrambled eggs with smoked haddock
## SERVES 1–2

**75 g/3 oz undyed smoked haddock**
**100 ml/3½ fl oz/scant ½ cup semi-skimmed milk**
**2 eggs**
**Freshly ground black pepper**
**A knob of sunflower margarine or low-fat spread, plus**
  **extra for spreading**
**1–2 slices of wholemeal bread**

① Cook the haddock in the milk for 2–3 minutes, until the flesh is beginning to flake. Strain and reserve the milk. Flake the haddock, discarding any skin and bones, and keep it warm.

② Beat the eggs with 15 ml/1 tbsp of the reserved milk and season with a little pepper. Melt a knob of sunflower margarine or low-fat spread in a small non-stick saucepan. Add the beaten eggs and stir briskly until the eggs are just set. Do not overcook.

③ Remove from the heat and stir in the flaked haddock.

④ Meanwhile, toast the bread, spread with sunflower margarine or low-fat spread and spoon the eggs on top.

PREPARATION AND COOKING TIME: 10 MINUTES

# Italian scrambled eggs
### SERVES 1–2

2 eggs
30 ml/2 tbsp semi-skimmed milk
Salt and freshly ground black pepper
15 ml/1 tbsp olive oil
½ small onion, chopped
3 button mushrooms, sliced
1 large tomato, chopped
25 g/1 oz peperoni sausage, chopped
A knob of sunflower margarine or low-fat spread,
    plus extra for spreading
1–2 slices of wholemeal bread

① Break the eggs into a bowl, add the milk and season with a pinch of salt and pepper. Beat well with a fork.

② Heat the oil in a frying pan (skillet) and gently fry (sauté) the onion and mushrooms for 3 minutes. Add the tomato and cook for 1 minute. Add the peperoni sausage.

③ Melt a knob of margarine or low-fat spread in a small saucepan and pour in the beaten eggs. Cook gently, stirring all the time, until thick and creamy.

④ Add the onion, mushrooms, tomato and peperoni to the eggs and mix gently together

⑤ Toast the bread and butter with sunflower margarine or low-fat spread. Serve with the scrambled eggs.

PREPARATION AND COOKING TIME: 10 MINUTES

# Bagels

*Toasted bagels make a change from ordinary toast. They are delicious with either sweet or savoury toppings. Try these ideas for breakfast.*

## Banana bagel:
Mash together 1 banana, 5 ml/1 tsp clear honey and a pinch of ground cinnamon. Halve a cinnamon bagel and toast the outer sides under the grill (broiler). Spread over the banana mixture and put back under the grill for 1–2 minutes. Top with a spoonful of plain, low-fat yoghurt.

## Dates and goat's cheese bagel:
Halve and toast a bagel. Spread the cut sides with goat's cheese and top with 3 or 4 chopped, stoned (pitted) dates and a few chopped walnuts. Drizzle a little clear honey over the top.

## Fresh fruit bagel:
Halve and toast a bagel. Spread some low-fat crème fraîche or fromage frais over each half and top with fresh fruit of your choice – try strawberries, raspberries, mango or kiwi fruit.

# English muffins
## MAKES 12

*Muffins are ideal for breakfast or a mid-morning snack. They freeze well, so you can make a batch and store them in the freezer. To serve, leave to thaw overnight, or defrost in a microwave, then warm them briefly in the oven.*

450 g/1 lb wholemeal flour
A pinch of salt
1 sachet of easy-blend dried yeast
25 g/1 oz/2 tbsp sunflower margarine or low-fat spread
150 ml/¼ pt/⅔ cup skimmed milk
150 ml/¼ pt/⅔ cup water
1 egg, beaten
50 g/2 oz/⅓ cup semolina (cream of wheat)

① Preheat the oven to 200°C/400°F/gas mark 6 and lightly grease a baking (cookie) sheet.

② Put the flour, salt and yeast into a mixing bowl. Stir thoroughly, then rub in the margarine or low-fat spread.

③ Heat the milk and water together until just lukewarm. Add to the flour with the beaten egg and mix to a dough.

④ Turn out on to a floured surface and knead well for 10 minutes, or work the dough in a food processor. Transfer to a lightly oiled bowl, cover with oiled clingfilm (plastic wrap) and leave to rise in a warm place for 45–50 minutes, until doubled in size.

⑤ Roll out the dough on a floured surface to 2 cm/¾ in thick. Stamp out 12 rounds with a 7.5 cm/3 in cutter.

⑥ Sprinkle the baking sheet with half the semolina and arrange the muffins on it. Sprinkle the remaining semolina over the top. Cover with oiled clingfilm and leave to rise in a warm place for 30 minutes.

⑦ Bake in the preheated oven for 15 minutes, until firm to the touch and hollow-sounding when tapped.

PREPARATION AND COOKING TIME: 40 MINUTES PLUS RISING

# Smoked salmon muffin
## SERVES 1

1 English muffin
25 g/1 oz/¼ cup low-fat cream cheese
5 ml/1 tsp lemon juice
15 ml/1 tbsp snipped fresh chives
Freshly ground black pepper
25 g/1 oz smoked salmon, thinly sliced

① Halve the muffin and toast it on both sides.

② Mix the cream cheese, lemon juice and chives together, and add plenty of freshly ground black pepper. Spread over the toasted muffin halves.

③ Top with the smoked salmon.

PREPARATION AND COOKING TIME: 5 MINUTES

# Bacon and egg muffin
## SERVES 1

1 egg
1 rasher (slice) of lean bacon
1 English muffin
1 tomato, sliced
Salt and freshly ground black pepper

① Bring a pan of lightly salted water to the boil, break in the egg and poach gently until the white is set.

② Meanwhile, grill (broil) the bacon rasher.

③ Halve and toast the muffin on both sides.

④ Arrange the bacon and sliced tomato on one half of the muffin. Top with the bacon and cooked egg. Season with a little salt and pepper, then top with the other muffin half.

PREPARATION AND COOKING TIME: 5 MINUTES

# *Avocado and bacon muffin*
## SERVES 1

1 rasher (slice) of lean bacon
1 small avocado
1 English muffin
5 ml/1 tsp lemon juice
Salt and freshly ground black pepper

① Cut the bacon into small pieces and fry (sauté) in its own fat until crisp.

② Peel, halve and stone (pit) the avocado. Mash half the flesh and slice the other half.

③ Halve and toast the muffin on both sides. Spread with the mashed avocado and top with the avocado slices.

④ Sprinkle over the lemon juice and season with a little salt and pepper.

⑤ Spoon the cooked bacon over the avocado, and eat immediately.

**PREPARATION AND COOKING TIME: 5 MINUTES**

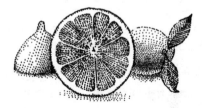

# Raisin and cinnamon muffins
## MAKES 6

75 g/3 oz/¾ cup sunflower margarine or low-fat spread
1 small egg
120 ml/4 fl oz/½ cup skimmed milk
150 g/5 oz/1¼ cups wholemeal flour
7.5 ml/1½ tsp baking powder
5 ml/1 tsp ground cinnamon
A pinch of salt
75 g/3 oz/½ cup raisins

① Preheat the oven to 190°C/375°F/gas mark 5.

② Grease six muffin tins (pans), or use paper cases (cupcake papers).

③ Put the margarine or spread, the egg and milk into a mixing bowl and beat well.

④ Sift the flour, baking powder, cinnamon and salt into the bowl. Fold in, then beat well. Fold in the raisins.

⑤ Divide the mixture between the tins and bake for 20 minutes, or until the muffins are well risen and firm to the touch.

⑥ Cool on a wire rack.

PREPARATION AND COOKING TIME: 30 MINUTES

## *Bacon and cornmeal muffins*
### MAKES 12

225 g/8 oz lean bacon rashers (slices), chopped
100 g/4 oz/1 cup sunflower margarine or low-fat spread
100 g/4 oz/1 cup plain (all-purpose) flour
15 ml/1 tbsp baking powder
5 ml/1 tsp caster (superfine) sugar (or artificial
  sweetener, if preferred)
A pinch of salt
225 g/8 oz/2 cups cornmeal
120 ml/4 fl oz/½ cup semi-skimmed milk
2 eggs, beaten

① Preheat the oven to 200°C/400°F/gas mark 6. Lightly grease 12 deep muffin tins (pans), or use paper cases (cupcake papers).

② Cook the bacon in a dry frying pan (skillet), without added fat, until crisp. Set aside.

③ Put the margarine or spread into a small saucepan over a gentle heat until melted – do not allow it to brown.

④ Sift the flour, baking powder, sugar or artificial sweetener and salt into a large mixing bowl. Stir in the cornmeal, then make a well in the centre.

⑤ Warm the milk, then lightly whisk in the eggs. Stir into the melted margarine or spread, then pour the mixture into the dry ingredients in the mixing bowl and stir until smooth. Stir in the cooked bacon.

⑥ Spoon the mixture into the greased tins or paper cases, half-filling each one.

⑦ Bake in the preheated oven for about 20 minutes, until well-risen and golden brown.

### PREPARATION AND COOKING TIME: 30 MINUTES

# Oatcakes
### MAKES 16

*These are delicious, spread with a little low-fat cream cheese.*

**350 g/12 oz/3 cups fine oatmeal**
**5 ml/1 tsp salt**
**A pinch of bicarbonate of soda (baking soda)**
**40 g/1½ oz/3 tbsp hard block margarine**
**150 ml/¼ pt/⅔ cup boiling water**

① Preheat the oven to 150°C/300°F/gas mark 2.

② Put the oatmeal, salt and bicarbonate of soda into a mixing bowl.

③ Cut the margarine into pieces and place in a separate bowl. Pour over the boiling water and stir until the margarine is melted. Add to the oatmeal and mix to a dough.

④ Turn out a surface dusted with oatmeal and knead lightly until smooth. Dust with oatmeal and roll out into two 25 cm/10 in rounds.

⑤ Cut each round into eight wedge-shapes and place on greased baking (cookie) sheets.

⑥ Bake in the preheated oven for 1 hour, until crisp, then transfer to a wire rack to cool.

PREPARATION AND COOKING TIME: 1 HOUR 10 MINUTES

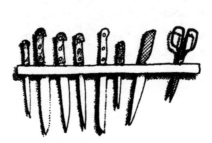

# Brack bread
### MAKES 8 SLICES

*A slice of this moist fruit loaf, spread with sunflower margarine or a low-fat spread, is ideal for a mid-morning snack or with afternoon tea.*

---

**450 g/1 lb/2⅔ cups dried mixed fruit**
**225 ml/8 fl oz/1 cup cold tea**
**250 g/8 oz/2 cups self-raising (self-rising) flour**
**1 egg, beaten**

---

① Put the dried fruit into a bowl, pour over the tea and leave to soak overnight.

② Next day, preheat the oven to 150°C/300°F/gas mark 2.

③ Mix together the fruit, flour and egg. Spoon into a well-greased and lined loaf tin (pan).

④ Bake for 2 hours. Turn out and leave to cool before cutting into slices.

   PREPARATION AND COOKING TIME: 2 HOURS PLUS SOAKING

# Banana bread

### MAKES 8 SLICES

100 g/4 oz/1 cup sunflower margarine or low-fat spread
5 ml/1 tsp bicarbonate of soda (baking soda)
225 g/8 oz/2 cups wholemeal flour
2 eggs, beaten
3 ripe bananas
45 ml/3 tbsp semi-skimmed milk
50 g/2 oz/½ cup sunflower seeds

① Preheat the oven to 180°C/350°F/gas mark 4. Grease and line a loaf tin (pan).

② Put the margarine or spread into a large bowl and beat until it is light and fluffy.

③ Stir the bicarbonate of soda into the flour, then add gradually to the creamed margarine or spread, alternating with the beaten eggs.

④ Peel and mash the bananas. Add to the cake mixture with the milk. Stir in the sunflower seeds.

⑤ Spoon the mixture into the prepared loaf tin and level the surface with a spoon. Bake for 1¼ to 1½ hours, until firm to the touch.

⑥ Cool on a wire rack and cut into slices for serving.

PREPARATION AND COOKING TIME:
1 HOUR 25 MINUTES TO 1 HOUR 40 MINUTES

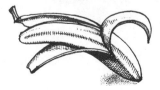

# *Pineapple and oat slice*
### MAKES 8 SLICES

**400 g/14 oz/1 large can of pineapple in natural juice**
**150 g/5 oz/1¼ cups porridge oats**
**5 ml/1 tsp ground cinnamon**
**150 ml/¼ pt/⅔ cup skimmed or semi-skimmed milk**

① Chop the pineapple finely and put into a mixing bowl. Add the juice, oats and cinnamon. Mix well.

② Add the milk, stir, and leave to stand for 30 minutes.

③ Meanwhile, preheat the oven to 190°C/375°F/gas mark 5. Grease an 18 cm/7 in sandwich tin (pan).

④ Spoon the mixture into the tin. Bake in the preheated oven for 1 to 1¼ hours, until golden and firm to the touch.

⑤ Allow to cool before turning out on to a wire rack.

PREPARATION AND COOKING TIME:
1½ HOURS PLUS 30 MINUTES STANDING

# Scones

## MAKES 12

*Scones (biscuits) are very quick and easy to make for a teatime treat. They are delicious served warm, halved and spread with a little sunflower margarine or low-fat spread.*

---

**450 g/1 lb/4 cups self-raising (self-rising) flour**
**A pinch of salt**
**10 ml/2 tsp baking powder**
**100 g/4 oz/1 cup sunflower margarine or low-fat spread**
**300 ml/½ pt/1¼ cups semi-skimmed milk**

---

① Preheat the oven to 220°C/425°F/gas mark 7.

② Sift the flour, salt and baking powder into a mixing bowl.

③ Using your fingertips, rub the margarine or spread into the flour mixture until it resembles breadcrumbs.

④ Add the milk and stir to make a soft dough.

⑤ Roll out the dough on a floured surface and cut into 12 rounds, using a pastry (cookie) cutter. Place on a greased baking (cookie) sheet.

⑥ Bake in the preheated oven for 8–10 minutes, until well-risen and lightly browned.

PREPARATION AND COOKING TIME: 20 MINUTES

# Fruit smoothie
## SERVES 1

*This makes a delicious alternative to tea or coffee.*

**50 g/2 oz fresh fruit, such as strawberries or raspberries, or 1 banana.**
**150 ml/¼ pt/⅔ cup plain low-fat yoghurt**
**5 ml/1 tsp clear honey**
**150 ml/¼ pt/⅔ cup cold semi-skimmed milk**

① Put all the ingredients into a food processor or liquidiser and blend until smooth.

② Spoon into a tall glass and drink immediately.

PREPARATION TIME: 3 MINUTES

# Banana cooler
## SERVES 1

*A refreshing breakfast drink with plenty of goodness as well – much better than tea or coffee.*

**1 banana, peeled**
**120 ml/4 fl oz/½ cup unsweetened orange juice**
**3 segments of pink grapefruit**
**45 ml/3 tbsp plain low-fat yoghurt**

① Put all the ingredients into a food processor or liquidiser and blend until smooth.

② Spoon into a tall glass and drink immediately.

PREPARATION TIME: 3 MINUTES

# Soups

*A*ll these soups include some carbohydrate in the form of pasta, pulses or potatoes. Serve them with pitta, wholemeal or multi-grain bread, and some fresh fruit to follow, to make a nutritious, well-balanced, light meal.

By adding herbs to flavour soups and other savoury dishes, you can cut down on the amount of salt you use. Coriander (cilantro), basil and parsley grow well in pots on the kitchen window sill; rosemary, sage, thyme, mint and chives need only a small space in the garden, or can be grown in outdoor pots. If you have no fresh herbs, dried herbs can be used, but remember to use only half the amount, as the flavour of dried herbs is very concentrated.

# Tomato soup with chick peas
## SERVES 4

*This soup is simplicity itself to make and the chick peas (garbanzos) provide an interesting flavour. Add some soup pasta for additional carbohydrate.*

---

**400 g/14 oz/1 large can of chick peas (garbanzos)**
**400 g/14 oz/1 large can of chopped tomatoes**
**30 ml/2 tbsp olive oil**
**1 clove of garlic, crushed**
**15 ml/1 tbsp tomato purée (paste)**
**750 ml/1¼ pts/3 cups vegetable stock**
**5 ml/1 tsp chopped fresh rosemary, or 2.5 ml/½ tsp dried**
**Salt and freshly ground black pepper**
**50 g/2 oz soup pasta**

---

① Drain the chick peas and purée them with the tomatoes in a blender or food processor.

② Heat the olive oil in a pan and gently fry (sauté) the garlic until it is soft but not brown. Add the puréed chick peas and tomatoes, the tomato purée, stock and rosemary. Season with a little salt and pepper.

③ Bring to the boil and simmer for 7 minutes.

④ Add the pasta and cook for a further 7 minutes.

PREPARATION AND COOKING TIME: 20 MINUTES

# Spicy lentil soup
### SERVES 4

30 ml/2 tbsp sunflower or vegetable oil
1 onion, peeled and chopped
1 garlic clove, crushed
5 ml/1 tsp cumin seeds
5 ml/1 tsp ground coriander
100 g/4 oz/⅔ cup red lentils
600 ml/1 pt/2½ cups vegetable stock
400 g/14 oz/1 large can of chopped tomatoes
Salt and freshly ground black pepper
15 ml/1 tbsp chopped fresh coriander (cilantro),
    to garnish
Warm pitta bread, to serve

① Heat the oil in a saucepan, add the onion and garlic and gently fry (sauté) for 3–4 minutes, until soft.

② Add the cumin seeds and cook for a further minute.

③ Add the ground coriander and lentils, stir well and cook gently for 2 minutes.

④ Add the vegetable stock and tomatoes, and season with a little salt and pepper.

⑤ Bring to the boil, then reduce the heat, cover and simmer for 45 minutes.

⑥ Garnish with chopped fresh coriander and serve with warm pitta bread.

PREPARATION AND COOKING TIME: 1 HOUR

# Minestrone soup
### SERVES 4

*Meaning 'big soup', minestrone is a meal in itself served with crusty Italian bread.*

---

15 ml/1 tbsp oil
1 onion, chopped
1 garlic clove, crushed
1 carrot, finely diced
2 courgettes (zucchini), chopped
15 ml/1 tbsp tomato purée (paste)
900 ml /1½ pts/3¾ cups beef stock
2.5 ml/½ tsp dried mixed herbs
400 g/14 oz/1 large can of cannellini or borlotti beans
50 g/2 oz soup pasta
50 g/2 oz/½ cup canned or frozen peas
Salt and freshly ground black pepper

---

① Heat the oil in a large saucepan. Add the onion, garlic, carrot and courgettes and cook gently for 5 minutes.

② Add the tomato purée, stock, dried herbs and beans.

③ Bring to the boil, cover and simmer for 10 minutes.

④ Add the pasta and peas and cook for a further 7 minutes, until the pasta is just cooked.

⑤ Check and adjust the seasoning if necessary.

⑥ Serve in warm bowls.

PREPARATION AND COOKING TIME: 25 MINUTES

# Winter vegetable soup
## SERVES 4

*You can vary the vegetables in the soup to include all your favourites and what you have available.*

50 g/2 oz/½ cup pot barley
1.2 litres/2 pts/5 cups vegetable stock
1 carrot, diced
1 small turnip or parsnip, diced
1 celery stick, chopped
1 onion, finely chopped
1 leek, trimmed and sliced
2.5 ml/½ tsp dried mixed herbs
1 bay leaf
30 ml/2 tbsp tomato purée (paste)
10 ml/2 tsp Worcester sauce
Salt and freshly ground black pepper
200 g/7 oz/1 small can of butter (lima) or borlotti beans

① Put the barley into a large saucepan with the stock. Bring to the boil, then cover and simmer for about 40 minutes, or until the barley is tender.

② Add the vegetables, herbs, tomato purée and Worcester sauce. Season with a little salt and pepper. Bring back to the boil, then reduce the heat, cover and simmer for 20 minutes.

③ Remove the bay leaf. Drain and rinse the beans and add to the soup. Simmer gently for 5 minutes.

④ Serve in warm bowls.

PREPARATION AND COOKING TIME: 1 HOUR 10 MINUTES

# *Mexican bean soup*
## SERVES 4

*Adjust the amount of chilli powder and Tabasco to make the soup milder or spicier.*

---

30 ml/2 tbsp olive oil
1 onion, chopped
1 garlic clove, crushed
1 green (bell) pepper, diced
375 g/12 oz tomatoes, chopped
2.5 ml/½ tsp chilli powder
900 ml/1½ pts/3¾ cups vegetable stock
30 ml/2 tbsp tomato purée (paste)
400 g/14 oz/1 large can of red kidney beans, drained
100 g/4 oz/1 cup canned or frozen sweetcorn (corn)
1 avocado, peeled, stoned (pitted) and diced
Salt and freshly ground black pepper
A little Tabasco sauce
15 ml/1 tbsp chopped fresh coriander (cilantro)
Corn chips, to serve

---

①  Heat the oil in a large saucepan and gently cook the onion until softened but not browned. Add the garlic, green pepper, tomatoes and chilli powder and cook for 3 minutes.

②  Add the stock, tomato purée, and three-quarters of the red kidney beans. Bring back to boil, then reduce the heat, cover and simmer for 30 minutes.

③  Purée the soup in a liquidiser or food processor.

④  Return the soup to the pan and add the remaining beans, the sweetcorn and avocado. Season with a little salt and pepper, and a few drops of Tabasco sauce. Reheat gently.

⑤  Stir in the coriander and serve with corn chips.

PREPARATION AND COOKING TIME: 45 MINUTES

# Sweetcorn chowder
### SERVES 4

30 ml/2 tbsp sunflower or vegetable oil
2 garlic cloves, crushed
1 onion, chopped
2 celery sticks, chopped
200 g/7 oz/1 small can of sweetcorn (corn)
200 g/7 oz/1 small can of butter (lima) beans
5 ml/1 tsp chopped fresh thyme
5 ml/1 tsp chopped fresh sage
5 ml/1 tsp chopped fresh basil
300 ml/½ pt/1¼ cups semi-skimmed milk
300 ml/½ pt/1¼ cups vegetable stock
Salt and freshly ground black pepper
Sprigs of thyme, to garnish

① Heat the oil in a large saucepan, add the garlic, onion and celery and cook gently for 5 minutes, until softened and the onion is translucent but not browned.

② Add the remaining ingredients and season with a little salt and pepper. Bring to the boil, then reduce the heat, cover and simmer for 10 minutes.

③ Serve garnished with sprigs of thyme.

### PREPARATION AND COOKING TIME: 15 MINUTES

# Squash and sweet potato soup
### SERVES 4

225 g/8 oz sweet potatoes, peeled and diced
225 g/8 oz butternut squash, peeled and diced
1 onion, chopped
2 garlic cloves, chopped
1 red chilli, seeded and finely chopped
900 ml/1½ pts/3¾ cups vegetable stock
300 ml/½ pt/1¼ cups dry white wine
Salt and freshly ground black pepper
15 ml/1 tbsp chopped fresh parsley or coriander
   (cilantro)

① Put the vegetables, stock and wine into a large saucepan. Bring to the boil, reduce the heat and simmer for 30 minutes, until all the vegetables are soft.

② Transfer the mixture to a food processor or liquidiser and process until smooth.

③ Return the soup to the saucepan and reheat gently. Check and adjust the seasoning if necessary.

④ Ladle the soup into warm bowls and serve sprinkled with chopped parsley or coriander.

### PREPARATION AND COOKING TIME: 40 MINUTES

# Split pea and ham soup
## SERVES 8

450 g/1 lb/2⅔ cups split green peas
100 g/4 oz lean bacon rashers (slices)
1 onion, chopped
1 garlic clove, crushed
1 carrot, sliced
1 celery stick, chopped
2 litres/3½ pts/8½ cups cold water
2 sprigs of thyme
2 bay leaves
225 g/8 oz potatoes, peeled and diced
1 knuckle of ham
Freshly ground black pepper

① Soak the split peas overnight in cold water, then drain through a sieve (strainer).

② Cut the bacon into small pieces and dry-fry in a large saucepan for 4–5 minutes, until crisp. Remove from the pan with a slotted spoon and set aside.

③ Add the onion, garlic, carrot and celery to the fat in the pan and cook for 3–4 minutes, until the onion is softened but not browned.

④ Return the bacon to the pan. Add the water, split peas, thyme, bay leaves, potato and knuckle of ham. Bring to the boil, reduce the heat, cover and simmer gently for 1 hour.

⑤ Remove the ham knuckle, thyme and bay leaves. Put the soup in batches in a food processor or liquidiser and blend until smooth. Pour into a clean pan.

⑥ Cut the ham meat from the knuckle, add to the soup and heat through gently. Season with plenty of freshly ground pepper before serving.

PREPARATION AND COOKING TIME: 1 HOUR 20 MINUTES PLUS SOAKING

# Salads

*A*ll the salads described here contain pasta, pulses or grains, so they are complete light meals in themselves, but you may want to supplement the carbohydrate by serving them with some wholemeal or multi-grain bread.

You can make your own salad dressing by mixing together 30 ml/2 tbsp olive oil, 15 ml/1 tbsp wine vinegar or lemon juice, a little sugar or artificial sweetener and mustard powder, salt and freshly ground black pepper. Put all the ingredients into a screw-topped jar and shake well before using.

# Potato, red pepper and chorizo salad
### SERVES 4

450 g/1 lb small new potatoes
30 ml/2 tbsp olive oil
1 red (bell) pepper, thinly sliced
1 small onion, finely chopped
50 g/2 oz chorizo sausage, chopped
Salt and freshly ground black pepper
15 ml/1 tbsp chopped fresh parsley
15 ml/1 tbsp snipped fresh chives

① Scrub the potatoes and cook in boiling, lightly salted water for about 10 minutes, until just soft.

② Heat 15 ml/1 tbsp of the oil in a frying pan (skillet) and cook the strips of pepper for 5–6 minutes, until soft.

③ Drain the potatoes and put into a serving bowl with the onion and chorizo.

④ Add the remaining oil to the cooked peppers and spoon over the potatoes. Season with a little salt and pepper. Toss together well.

⑤ Sprinkle over the herbs.

### PREPARATION AND COOKING TIME: 15 MINUTES

# Three-bean and nut salad
## SERVES 4

225 g/8 oz French (green) beans
400 g/14 oz/1 large can of red kidney beans
400 g/14 oz/1 large can of cannellini beans
6–8 spring onions (scallions), chopped
3 garlic cloves, finely chopped
30 ml/2 tbsp chopped fresh parsley
50 g/2 oz/½ cup cashew nuts or walnuts
60 ml/4 tbsp French dressing

① Cook the French beans in boiling, lightly salted water for 5–6 minutes, until tender but still with some 'bite'. Drain and chop into short pieces.

② Drain and rinse the kidney and cannellini beans.

③ Put all the beans into a serving bowl with the spring onions, garlic, parsley and nuts. Spoon over the French dressing and toss well to mix.

PREPARATION AND COOKING TIME: 10 MINUTES

# Red bean and feta cheese salad
### SERVES 4

2 × 400 g/14 oz/large cans of red kidney beans
2 garlic cloves, crushed
1 onion, finely chopped
4 tomatoes, chopped
30 ml/2 tbsp chopped fresh mixed herbs
15 ml/1 tbsp wine vinegar
30 ml/2 tbsp oil
Salt and freshly ground black pepper
150 g/6 oz/1½ cups Feta cheese, crumbled

① Put the beans, garlic, onion, tomatoes and herbs into a large serving bowl.

② Pour over the vinegar and oil.

③ Season with a little salt and pepper.

④ Sprinkle the Feta cheese over the top, then serve.

PREPARATION TIME: 5 MINUTES

## Bean, tuna and anchovy salad
### SERVES 4

2 × 200 g/7 oz/small cans of tuna, drained and flaked
2 × 400 g/14 oz/large cans of cannellini beans, drained
1 small red onion, sliced into rings
50 g/2 oz/1 small can of anchovy fillets
45 ml/3 tbsp olive oil
15 ml/1 tbsp lemon juice
Salt and freshly ground black pepper
15 ml/1 tbsp chopped fresh parsley

① Put the tuna, beans and onion rings into a serving bowl.

② Rinse the anchovies under cold, running water to remove excess salt and pat dry with kitchen paper (paper towels). Chop and add to the salad.

③ Mix together the olive oil and lemon juice, and season with a little salt and pepper. Pour over the salad and toss lightly.

④ Sprinkle over the chopped parsley.

PREPARATION TIME: 10 MINUTES

# Chicken, lentil and rocket salad

### SERVES 4

175 g/6 oz/1½ cups green lentils
45 ml/3 tbsp sunflower oil
30 ml/2 tbsp lemon juice
5 ml/1 tsp Dijon mustard
Salt and freshly ground black pepper
225 g/8 oz rocket leaves
225 g/8 oz/2 cups cooked chicken, cubed
50 g/2 oz flaked (slivered) almonds, toasted

① Rinse and drain the lentils. Put into a saucepan with plenty of fresh, cold water, bring to the boil and boil rapidly for 10 minutes. Lower the heat and simmer for a further 20 minutes, or until tender. Drain.

② Mix the oil, lemon juice and mustard with a little salt and pepper and stir the dressing into the cooked lentils.

③ Arrange the rocket leaves in a serving dish, and spoon the lentil mixture into the centre.

④ Arrange the chicken round the edge of the lentils and sprinkle over the toasted almonds.

### PREPARATION AND COOKING TIME: 35 MINUTES

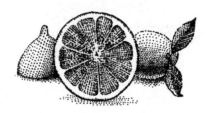

# *Prawn, avocado and pasta salad*
### SERVES 4

225 g/8 oz pasta shapes
1 avocado, peeled, stoned (pitted) and sliced
15 ml/1 tbsp lemon juice
225 g/8 oz cooked peeled prawns (shrimp)
30 ml/2 tbsp reduced-fat mayonnaise
30 ml/2 tbsp plain low-fat yoghurt
1 garlic clove, crushed
15 ml/1 tbsp snipped fresh chives
Freshly ground black pepper
225 g/8 oz rocket or baby spinach leaves

① Cook the pasta in plenty of boiling, lightly salted water for 10–12 minutes, or according to the packet instructions. Drain and rinse under cold, running water.

② Toss the avocado in the lemon juice, then add to the pasta with the prawns.

③ Mix together the mayonnaise, yoghurt, garlic and chives, and season with pepper. Fold into the pasta.

④ Arrange the rocket or spinach leaves in a serving bowl and spoon the pasta mixture on top.

PREPARATION AND COOKING TIME: 15 MINUTES

# Beansprout and egg noodle salad
### SERVES 4

350 g/12 oz egg noodles
15 ml/1 tbsp sesame seeds
2 carrots, grated
225 g/8 oz beansprouts
100 g/4 oz baby spinach leaves, shredded
6–8 spring onions (scallions), finely sliced
15 ml/1 tbsp chopped fresh coriander (cilantro) or parsley
15 ml/1 tbsp chilli sauce
15 ml/1 tbsp sesame oil
30 ml/2 tbsp soy sauce

① Put the noodles into a large pan of boiling, lightly salted water. Bring back to the boil and simmer for 4 minutes. Drain, rinse in cold water and put into a serving bowl.

② Heat a small frying pan (skillet) and toast the sesame seeds for 2 minutes.

③ Add the vegetables, herbs, chilli sauce, sesame oil and soy sauce to the noodles and toss well.

④ Sprinkle with toasted sesame seeds before serving.

PREPARATION AND COOKING TIME: 10 MINUTES

# *Fruited bulghar salad*
## SERVES 4

225 g/8 oz/2 cups bulghar (cracked wheat)
6–8 spring onions (scallions)
100 g/4 oz cucumber, diced
1 mango, peeled, stoned (pitted) and chopped
1 avocado, peeled, stoned and chopped
50 g/2 oz/⅓ cup raisins
50 g/2 oz/½ cup walnuts, chopped
30 ml/2 tbsp chopped fresh coriander (cilantro)
30 ml/2 tbsp sesame seeds
30 ml/2 tbsp sunflower seeds
45 ml/3 tbsp olive oil
30 ml/2 tbsp lemon juice
Salt and freshly ground black pepper
Mixed salad leaves

① Put the bulghar in a bowl, cover with boiling water and set aside for 15–20 minutes, until all the water has absorbed and the bulghar is soft. Drain off any surplus liquid.

② Put the bulghar into a large serving bowl and add the spring onions, cucumber, mango, avocado, raisins, walnuts and coriander.

③ Toast the seeds in a dry frying pan (skillet) and add to the bulghar mixture.

④ Add the olive oil and lemon juice, and season with a little salt and pepper. Toss well to mix.

⑤ Arrange the salad leaves in a serving dish and spoon the bulghar salad on top.

PREPARATION AND COOKING TIME: 20–25 MINUTES

# Lentil and basmati rice salad

## SERVES 4

100 g/4 oz/⅔ cup green lentils
225 g/8 oz/1 cup basmati rice
60 ml/4 tbsp French dressing
2 carrots, grated
½ cucumber, grated
4–5 spring onions (scallions), chopped
45 ml/3 tbsp chopped fresh parsley

① Soak the lentils in cold water for 30 minutes. Drain, then boil rapidly in fresh water for 20–25 minutes until soft. Drain thoroughly.

② Meanwhile, cook the basmati rice in plenty of boiling, lightly salted water for 10 minutes. Drain.

③ Put the cooked lentils and rice into a large bowl and stir in the dressing. Leave to cool.

④ Add the carrots, cucumber, onions and parsley and mix together well.

PREPARATION AND COOKING TIME:
30 MINUTES PLUS SOAKING AND COOLING

# Lentil and tomato salad
### SERVES 4

**225 g/8 oz/1⅓ cups green lentils**
**75 ml/5 tbsp French dressing**
**4 spring onions (scallions), chopped**
**4 tomatoes, chopped**
**2 celery sticks, chopped**
**15 ml/1 tbsp chopped fresh parsley**
**Salt and freshly ground black pepper**
**1 round lettuce, separated into leaves**

① Soak the lentils for 30 minutes in cold water. Drain, then boil in fresh water for 20–25 minutes until soft. Drain thoroughly and mix with the French dressing while still warm. Leave to cool.

② Add the spring onions, tomatoes, celery and parsley and season with salt and pepper.

③ Arrange the lettuce leaves in a salad bowl and spoon the lentil mixture in the centre.

PREPARATION AND COOKING TIME:
30 MINUTES PLUS SOAKING AND COOLING

# fruited brown rice salad
### SERVES 4

225 g/8 oz/1 cup brown rice
4–5 spring onions (scallions), chopped
1 garlic clove, crushed
5 ml/1 tsp finely chopped fresh root ginger
1 red (bell) pepper, chopped
50 g/2 oz/⅓ cup raisins
50 g/2 oz/½ cup cashew nuts
60 ml/4 tbsp soy sauce
60 ml/4 tbsp French dressing
30 ml/2 tbsp chopped fresh parsley

① Cook the rice in plenty of boiling, lightly salted water for 40–45 minutes, until tender. Drain, rinse and leave to cool.

② Put the cooled rice into a large serving bowl and add all the other ingredients. Toss well before serving.

PREPARATION AND COOKING TIME: 50 MINUTES PLUS COOLING

# *Apricot and nut wholewheat salad*
## SERVES 4

150 g/6 oz/1½ cups wholewheat grains
3 celery sticks, chopped
75 g/3 oz/½ cup dried apricots, chopped
50 g/2 oz/½ cup brazil nuts, chopped
25 g/1 oz/¼ cup unsalted peanuts
30 ml/2 tbsp olive oil
15 ml/1 tbsp lemon juice
15 ml/1 tbsp chopped fresh parsley
Mixed leaf salad, to serve

① Put the wholewheat grain into a bowl with plenty of cold water and soak overnight.

② Drain and tip into a large saucepan of boiling water. Simmer gently for about 25 minutes, until the grains are tender but still have a little 'bite'. Drain into a colander and rinse under cold running water. Place in a serving bowl.

③ Add the celery, apricots and nuts to the wholewheat. Stir well to mix.

④ Mix the olive oil and lemon juice together. Season well and pour over the salad. Toss well.

⑤ Sprinkle over the chopped parsley, then serve with a mixed leaf salad.

PREPARATION AND COOKING TIME: 35 MINUTES PLUS SOAKING

# Egg dishes

*I*f you keep a few eggs in the fridge you need never be at a loss for ideas for a quick meal. Eggs have a high food value – they contain protein, as well as vitamins A, B and D, iron and calcium in the yolk. However, they do also contain cholesterol, so it is recommended that you don't eat more than one or two per week.

The egg dishes described here are all substantial enough for a filling meal, eaten with some wholemeal or multi-grain bread or toast and perhaps a small green salad.

# Spinach and herb frittata
## SERVES 2

15 ml/1 tbsp olive oil
1 leek, washed and finely chopped
100 g/4 oz fresh spinach, washed and finely shredded
4 eggs
25 g/1 oz goat's cheese
30 ml/2 tbsp chopped fresh parsley
30 ml/2 tbsp snipped fresh chives
Freshly ground black pepper

① Heat the oil in a large frying pan (skillet). Add the chopped leek and fry (sauté) gently for 3–4 minutes.

② Add the shredded spinach and cook for a further 2–3 minutes, until the spinach has wilted.

③ Break the eggs into a bowl, add the goat's cheese, herbs and pepper. Beat gently to mix.

④ Pour the egg mixture into the frying pan and cook slowly over a low heat for 4–5 minutes, until set underneath but still moist in the centre.

⑤ Preheat the grill (broiler) to moderate. Place the frying pan under the grill and cook until the top is slightly browned.

PREPARATION AND COOKING TIME: 15 MINUTES

# *Pimiento and sweetcorn omelette*

### SERVES 2

15 ml/1 tbsp olive oil
1 small onion, sliced
1 garlic clove, crushed
50 g/2 oz/½ cup canned or cooked frozen sweetcorn
  (corn)
50 g/2 oz canned pimientos, drained and sliced
50 g/2 oz/½ cup cooked frozen peas
1 potato, cooked and diced
25 g/1 oz chorizo sausage, sliced
4 eggs
Salt and freshly ground black pepper

① Heat the oil in a frying pan (skillet), add the onion and garlic and cook gently for 5–6 minutes, until soft.

② Add the sweetcorn, pimientos, peas, potato and sausage. Stir well to mix.

③ Beat the eggs, season with a little salt and pepper and pour over the vegetables. Cook gently until the egg is set, but still a little moist.

④ Slide the frying pan under a hot grill (broiler) for a few minutes to cook the top of the omelette.

### PREPARATION AND COOKING TIME: 15 MINUTES

# flamenco eggs
### SERVES 2

30 ml/2 tbsp olive oil
1 small onion, sliced
1 red (bell) pepper, cut into strips
75 g/3 oz bacon, cut into strips
1 potato, cooked and diced
50 g/2 oz/½ cup cooked frozen peas
2 tomatoes, chopped
15 ml/1 tbsp chopped fresh parsley
Salt and freshly ground black pepper
2 eggs

① Preheat the oven to 180°C/350°F/gas mark 4.

② Heat the oil in a frying pan (skillet), add the onion, pepper and bacon and fry (sauté) gently for 5–6 minutes.

③ Add the potato and cook until lightly browned.

④ Add the peas, tomatoes and parsley. Season to taste with a little salt and pepper.

⑤ Turn the vegetable mixture into a shallow, ovenproof dish. Using a spoon, press two hollows in the mixture and break an egg into each one.

⑥ Cook in the preheated oven for 15 minutes, until the egg whites are just set.

⑦ Serve immediately.

PREPARATION AND COOKING TIME: 30 MINUTES

# Eggs Florentine
SERVES 2

**4 eggs**
**225 g/8 oz/1 small packet of frozen spinach**
*For the cheese sauce:*
**25 g/1 oz/2 tbsp sunflower margarine or low-fat spread**
**25 g/1 oz/¼ cup plain (all-purpose) flour**
**225 ml/8 fl oz/1 cup semi-skimmed milk**
**50 g/2 oz/½ cup reduced-fat Cheddar cheese, grated**
**2.5 g/½ tsp made mustard**
**Salt and freshly ground black pepper**

① Cook the eggs in boiling water for 8 minutes. Plunge into cold water and remove the shells.

② Meanwhile, cook the spinach according to the instructions on the packet.

③ To make the cheese sauce, melt the margarine or spread in a saucepan and stir in the flour. Remove the pan from the heat and gradually stir in the milk, making sure there are no lumps. Return the pan to the heat and bring the sauce to the boil, stirring all the time until thickened.

④ Remove the sauce from the heat, stir in the cheese and mustard, and season to taste.

⑤ Put the spinach into a flameproof dish and arrange the eggs on top. Pour over the cheese sauce.

⑥ Brown under a hot grill (broiler) for a couple of minutes.

PREPARATION AND COOKING TIME: 15 MINUTES

# Eggs and leeks au gratin
### SERVES 2

**4 eggs**
**25 g/1 oz/2 tbsp sunflower margarine or low-fat spread**
**4 leeks, chopped**
*For the cheese sauce:*
**25 g/1 oz/1 oz sunflower margarine or low-fat spread**
**25 g/1 oz/¼ cup plain (all-purpose) flour**
**225 ml/8 fl oz/1 cup semi-skimmed milk**
**50 g/2 oz/½ cup reduced-fat Cheddar cheese, grated**
**2.5 g/½ tsp made mustard**
**Salt and freshly ground black pepper**

① Cook the eggs in boiling water for 8 minutes. Plunge into cold water and remove the shells.

② Melt the margarine or spread in a frying pan (skillet) and cook the leeks gently for 5 minutes.

③ To make the cheese sauce, melt the margarine or spread in a saucepan and stir in the flour. Remove the pan from the heat and gradually stir in the milk, stirring to remove any lumps. Return the pan to the heat and bring the sauce to the boil, stirring all the time until thickened.

④ Stir in half the cheese and the mustard and season to taste.

⑤ Put the leeks into a flameproof dish. Halve the eggs and arrange on top of the leeks, rounded-side up. Pour over the cheese sauce. Sprinkle the remaining grated cheese on top.

⑥ Put under a hot grill (broiler) until browned.

PREPARATION AND COOKING TIME: 20 MINUTES

# Egg and salmon toast

### SERVES 1

50 g/2 oz/½ cup reduced-fat Cheddar cheese, grated
100 g/4 oz/1 small can of salmon, drained and mashed
15 ml/1 tbsp plain low-fat yoghurt
15 ml/1 tbsp lemon juice
Salt and freshly ground black pepper
Paprika, to taste
1 egg, beaten
2 slices of wholemeal bread

① Put the grated cheese, salmon, yoghurt and lemon juice in a mixing bowl. Season with salt, pepper and paprika to taste. Mix well, then beat in the egg.

② Toast the bread and place in a flameproof dish. Spoon the cheese mixture on top of the toast.

③ Place under a preheated low grill (broiler) for 10 minutes to heat through, then increase the heat and grill for another 5 minutes to brown the top.

PREPARATION AND COOKING TIME: 15 MINUTES

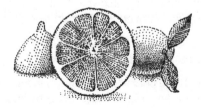

# Salmon and cottage cheese quiche
## SERVES 4–6

*You can make pastry (paste) using only wholemeal flour if you prefer, but adding a little white flour makes it lighter. Choose a polyunsaturated margarine or low-fat spread spread that is suitable for cooking.*

100 g/4 oz/1 cup wholemeal flour
50 g/2 oz/½ cup plain (all-purpose) flour
A pinch of salt
75 g/3 oz/¾ cup sunflower margarine or low-fat spread
200 g/7 oz/1 medium can of pink salmon, drained
100 g/4 oz/1 cup low-fat cottage cheese, drained
2 eggs, lightly beaten
30 ml/2 tbsp skimmed or semi-skimmed milk
Freshly ground black pepper
1 tomato, sliced

① To make the pastry, sift the flours and salt into a mixing bowl. Rub in the fat until the mixture resembles breadcrumbs, then stir in just enough cold water to bind the mixture into a soft but not sticky dough. Chill for 30 minutes in the fridge.

② Preheat the oven to 200°C/400°F/gas mark 6.

③ On a floured surface, roll the pastry into a round and place in a 26 cm/10 in flan tin (pie pan). Prick a few holes in the bottom of the pastry case (pie shell), line with foil and bake in the preheated oven for 10 minutes.

④ Flake the salmon, discard any skin and bones and spread over the bottom of the pastry case.

⑤ Put the cottage cheese, eggs and milk into a food processor or liquidiser and blend until smooth. Season with pepper and pour over the salmon. Arrange the tomato slices decoratively on top.

⑥ Bake for 30–35 minutes, or until the filling mixture is firm.

PREPARATION AND COOKING TIME: 50 MINUTES PLUS CHILLING

# Tomato and egg tagine
## SERVES 2

4 eggs
300 ml/½ pt/1¼ cups boiling water
15 ml/1 tbsp olive oil
1 garlic clove, crushed
4–5 spring onions (scallions), chopped
225 g/8 oz tomatoes, chopped
225 g/8 oz/2 cups quick-cook couscous
Salt and freshly ground black pepper
5 ml/1 tsp ground cumin

① Cook two of the eggs in boiling water for 5–6 minutes. Drain and cover with cold water until cool enough to handle. Peel and roughly chop the eggs.

② Heat the oil in a pan and add the garlic and spring onions. Cook gently for 5 minutes, then add the tomatoes. Continue cooking for a further 10 minutes, stirring gently occasionally.

③ Meanwhile, put the couscous in a bowl and pour over the boiling water. Soak for about 5 minutes, stirring occasionally.

④ Beat the remaining eggs and add to the tomato mixture in the pan. Season with a pinch of salt, pepper and cumin. Stir and allow to cook gently for 2–3 minutes, until the egg is not quite set.

⑤ Add the chopped egg and cook for 1 further minute.

⑥ Serve immediately with the couscous.

PREPARATION AND COOKING TIME: 20 MINUTES

# Eggs tonnato
### SERVES 2

4 eggs
200 g/7 oz/1 small can of tuna
75 ml/5 tbsp low-fat mayonnaise
1 small onion, finely chopped
30 ml/2 tbsp chopped fresh parsley
Salt and freshly ground black pepper

①  Put the eggs into a small saucepan, cover with water and bring to the boil. Reduce the heat and simmer for 8–10 minutes.

②  Shell the eggs and halve them. Arrange flat-side down in a shallow dish.

③  Drain the tuna, flake it, and add to the mayonnaise.

④  Stir in the onion and half the parsley.

⑤  Season to taste with a little salt and pepper.

⑥  Spoon the tuna over the eggs, and sprinkle with the remaining parsley.

### PREPARATION AND COOKING TIME: 15 MINUTES

# fast food

When you need a meal in a hurry, you may be tempted to buy a ready-to-cook meal or other convenience food from the supermarket, but these can be high in fat, sugar and salt, and don't necessarily include the right amount of carbohydrate. This section contains a selection of quick, tasty and healthy light meals that are ideal for those occasions when you don't have time to spend in the kitchen. If you do buy ready-prepared meals, make sure you always read the contents label, and add some extra carbohydrate, vegetables or salad, if necessary.

# Sandwich fillings

*A sandwich made with wholemeal or multi-grain bread, spread with a little sunflower margarine or a low-fat spread and filled with a suitable filling, makes an excellent lunch for working days, or days when you don't want to cook. Here are some suggestions for fillings.*

### Egg mayonnaise and chives:
Hard-boil (hard-cook) an egg, remove the shell and mash with enough low-fat mayonnaise to make a creamy filling. Add plenty of snipped, fresh chives.

### Chicken, walnuts and watercress or rocket:
Shred some cooked chicken and finely chop some walnuts. Mix with 15 ml/1 tbsp low-fat mayonnaise and some freshly ground black pepper. Spoon on to the bread and top with watercress or rocket leaves.

### Bacon, lettuce and tomato:
Grill (broil) a couple of lean bacon rashers (slices) until crisp. Lay the bacon on the bread and top with crisp, shredded lettuce and thinly sliced tomato. Add 5 ml/1 tsp low-fat mayonnaise, if liked.

### Bacon and avocado:
Cut a couple of lean bacon rashers (slices) into small pieces and dry-fry them until crisp. Peel half an avocado and mash with a little lemon juice. Spread over the bread and top with the cooked bacon.

### Cream cheese, toasted sunflower seeds and lettuce:
Toss 15 ml/1 tbsp sunflower seeds in a dry frying pan (skillet) to toast them. Spread some low-fat cream cheese on the bread, press the sunflower seeds into it, and cover with a layer of crisp, shredded lettuce.

### Cream cheese with sun-dried tomato and basil:
Chop some sun-dried tomato and fresh basil leaves, and mix with low-fat cream cheese. Top with crisp, shredded lettuce.

**Cottage cheese, apple and cashew nuts:**
Grate a small eating (dessert) apple and mix with the cottage cheese. Add a few unsalted cashew nuts.

**Tuna, mayonnaise and cucumber:**
Mash canned tuna with 15 ml/1 tbsp low-fat mayonnaise. Grate in some cucumber and season well with pepper.

**Sardine and tomato:**
Mash 3–4 canned sardines and spread on to the bread. Top with thinly sliced tomato.

**Salmon, fromage frais and spring onions:**
Mash some canned salmon with 15 ml/1 tbsp low-fat fromage frais, then stir in some chopped spring onions (scallions).

# Stuffed ciabatta
### SERVES 2

*Ciabatta is an Italian bread made with olive oil and garlic, sometimes flavoured with sun-dried tomatoes and basil. It makes tasty sandwiches, or you can stuff it with a wonderful hot vegetable filling. You can also add all kinds of different toppings to make Bruschetta (see page 69).*

½ ciabatta loaf
2 small courgettes (zucchini), thinly sliced
1 red onion, thinly sliced
1 red (bell) pepper, thinly sliced
15 ml/1 tbsp olive oil
30 ml/2 tbsp low-fat crème fraîche
5 ml/1 tsp pesto

① Cut the ciabatta in half lengthways.

② Place the vegetables on a baking sheet, drizzle over the olive oil and put under a hot grill (broiler) for about 7 minutes, until tender and slightly charred.

③ Mix together the crème fraîche and pesto and spread over the cut sides of the bread.

④ Top with the vegetables and sandwich together.

PREPARATION AND COOKING TIME: 8 MINUTES

# *Bruschetta*

### SERVES 2

½ **ciabatta loaf**
1 **tomato, chopped**
15 ml/1 **tbsp chopped fresh parsley**
2–3 **spring onions (scallions), chopped**
**Salt and freshly ground black pepper**
45 ml/3 **tbsp olive oil**
1 **garlic clove, crushed**
100 g/4 **oz mushrooms**
30 ml/2 **tbsp white wine**

① Cut the ciabatta in half lengthways.

② Mix together the tomato, parsley and spring onions. Season with a little salt and pepper.

③ Mix the olive oil with the garlic. Put the mushrooms on a grill (broiler) tray and brush with the olive oil mixture. Sprinkle with wine and grill (broil) for 4–5 minutes, until cooked through. Remove from the grill.

④ Brush the remaining olive oil mixture over the pieces of ciabatta bread and toast under the grill.

⑤ Arrange the mushrooms on the toasted ciabatta and spoon the tomato mixture on top. Place under the hot grill for 1–2 minutes.

PREPARATION AND COOKING TIME: 10 MINUTES

# Hummus
## SERVES 4–6

*This makes an excellent quick lunch, served with pitta bread
and a fresh green salad.*

---

200 g/7 oz/1 small can of chick peas (garbanzos)
30 ml/2 tbsp tahini
2 garlic cloves, crushed
30 ml/2 tbsp olive oil
Juice of ½ lemon
60 ml/4 tbsp plain low-fat yoghurt
Freshly ground black pepper
A little paprika, for dusting

---

① Drain the chick peas and put into a food processor or liquidiser with the tahini, garlic, olive oil, lemon juice and yoghurt. Blend to a soft creamy purée.

② Season with pepper, and spoon into a serving dish. Sprinkle with paprika.

PREPARATION TIME: 5 MINUTES

# Tuna-stuffed pitta
## SERVES 1

---

90 g/3½ oz/1 very small can of tuna
5 ml/1 tsp low-fat mayonnaise
2 crisp lettuce leaves, shredded
1 tomato, sliced
3–4 slices of cucumber
1 pitta bread

---

① Drain the tuna and mix well with the mayonnaise.

② Toast the pitta bread, then use a sharp knife to open along one side.

③ Spoon in the tuna mayonnaise, then add the lettuce, tomato and cucumber.

PREPARATION TIME: 5 MINUTES

# Tabbouleh-stuffed pitta
### SERVES 1

**50 g/2 oz/½ cup bulghar (cracked wheat)**
**2–3 cherry tomatoes**
**2–3 spring onions (scallions)**
**50 g/2 oz cucumber, finely chopped**
**15 ml/1 tbsp chopped fresh parsley**
**15 ml/1 tbsp chopped fresh mint**
**10 ml/2 tsp lemon juice**
**10 ml/2 tsp olive oil**
**Salt and freshly ground black pepper**
**1 pitta bread**

① Put the bulghar into a small bowl, cover with boiling water and leave to soak for 15 minutes, or until the grains are tender. Drain off any surplus liquid.

② Mix the bulghar with the other ingredients, and season with a little salt and pepper.

③ Toast the pitta bread, then use a sharp knife to open along one side. Stuff the tabbouleh into the pitta bread.

PREPARATION TIME: 5 MINUTES PLUS SOAKING

# Pitta pizza
### SERVES 1

**1 pitta bread**
**1 tomato, sliced**
**1 slice of ham**
**1 slice of reduced-fat Cheddar cheese**
**2.5 ml/½ tsp dried mixed herbs**

① Put the pitta on a grill (broiler) rack. Arrange the sliced tomato, ham and cheese on top. Sprinkle over the herbs.

② Cook under a hot grill until the cheese is bubbling.

PREPARATION AND COOKING TIME: 10 MINUTES

# Chicken-stuffed pitta
### SERVES 1

---

15 ml/1 tbsp sunflower or vegetable oil
50 g/2 oz/½ cup diced cooked chicken
75 g/3 oz button mushrooms, sliced
½ small red (bell) pepper, sliced
2.5 ml/½ tsp chilli seasoning
15 ml/1 tbsp soy sauce
2.5 ml/½ tsp sugar
Freshly ground black pepper
1 carrot, peeled and grated
50 g/2 oz cabbage, finely sliced
1 pitta bread

---

① Heat the oil in a frying pan (skillet) and fry (sauté) the chicken, mushrooms and red pepper for about 2 minutes, stirring occasionally.

② Mix the chilli seasoning with the soy sauce and sugar, and plenty of pepper. Add to the chicken with the carrot and cabbage. Cook over a high heat for 2 minutes, stirring all the time.

③ Meanwhile, put the pitta bread in a toaster or under a moderate grill (broiler) to warm.

④ Make a slit along one edge of the pitta and open up to form a pocket. Fill with the chicken and vegetable mixture.

PREPARATION TIME: 10 MINUTES

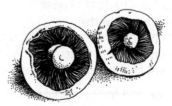

# Baked potatoes

*A baked potato with a tasty topping, served with a green salad, makes an ideal quick, satisfying and balanced meal. Choose a potato with an unblemished skin, weighing about 200 g/7 oz, and prick the skin in several places. For the best flavour, bake in a preheated oven at 180°C/350°F/gas mark 4 for 1 hour, but for a really speedy snack, wrap the potato in kitchen paper (paper towels) and cook in the microwave on High for 5–7 minutes.*

Try these toppings:

◇ Canned baked beans

◇ Canned chilli beans

◇ Chilli con carne (see page 101)

◇ Poached egg

◇ Sardines

◇ Low-fat cottage cheese, grated apple and unsalted peanuts

◇ Low-fat cream cheese, sun-dried tomato and chopped, fresh basil

◇ Crisp grilled (broiled) lean bacon, lettuce and tomato

◇ Tuna, chopped spring onions (scallions) and low-fat mayonnaise

◇ Smoked salmon, low-fat fromage frais and snipped fresh chives

◇ Cooked peeled prawns (shrimp) and low-fat crème fraîche

◇ Canned sweetcorn (corn) and chopped, grilled (broiled) bacon

◇ Chopped ham, chopped celery, chopped, unsalted nuts and plain, low-fat yoghurt

# Seafood main meals

*F*ish is extremely nutritious: it is a good source of protein, vitamins and minerals, particularly iodine. Canned fish with edible bones, such as sardines and mackerel, also provide calcium.

Oily fish in particular – herring, mackerel, tuna, salmon – are rich in health-giving omega-3 fatty acids, but all fish is low in the harmful, saturated fats that are found in red meat. Research suggests that eating fish two or three times a week may help to lower the level of cholesterol in the blood and so help to protect against heart disease.

There is a wide variety of fish and shellfish available, and many different ways of cooking it. Grilling (broiling) and poaching are the simplest and quickest ways of preparing fish – but if you want something more adventurous there are lots of recipes in this section for you to try.

I have also included some ideas for vegetables to accompany your fish dishes, but these are suggestions only – cook whatever is fresh and in season, or suits your own family's tastes and preferences.

# Herrings in oatmeal
## SERVES 4

*Herring are rich in omega-3 fatty acids, which help protect against coronary heart disease. Oats are high in soluble fibre and an excellent food for people with diabetes.*

**4 herrings**
**Salt and freshly ground black pepper**
**100 g/4 oz/1 cup oatmeal**
**30 ml/2 tbsp sunflower or vegetable oil**
**Lemon wedges, to garnish**
**New potatoes, broccoli and carrots, to serve**

① Cut the heads off the fish, clean them and remove the backbones. Rinse thoroughly under cold, running water and pat dry with kitchen paper (paper towels).

② Sprinkle the fish with a little salt and pepper. Coat with the oatmeal, pressing it well in.

③ Heat the oil in a large frying pan (skillet). Add the fish and fry (sauté) for about 5 minutes on each side. Drain on kitchen paper.

④ Garnish with lemon wedges and serve hot with new potatoes, broccoli and carrots.

PREPARATION AND COOKING TIME: 15 MINUTES

## *Mackerel with mustard and oats*
### SERVES 4

**550 g/1¼ lb mackerel fillets**
**10 ml/2 tsp lemon juice**
**Salt and freshly ground black pepper**
**50 g/2 oz/½ cup porridge oats**
**15 ml/1 tbsp Dijon mustard**
**Chopped fresh parsley and slices of lemon, to garnish**
**New potatoes and green vegetables, to serve**

① Place the mackerel on a grill (broiler) rack lined with foil. Sprinkle with lemon juice and a little salt and pepper.

② Mix the oats and mustard together and spread over the mackerel. Cook under a medium grill for 10–15 minutes, or until the flesh flakes.

③ Garnish with parsley and slices of lemon. Serve with new potatoes and green vegetables.

PREPARATION AND COOKING TIME: 15 MINUTES

# Plaice in paprika and mushroom sauce
### SERVES 4

4 plaice fillets
300 ml/½ pt/1¼ cups semi-skimmed milk
Salt and freshly ground black pepper
25 g/1 oz/2 tbsp sunflower margarine or low-fat spread
50 g/2 oz button mushrooms, sliced
15 g/½ oz/2 tbsp plain (all-purpose) flour
10–15 ml/2–3 tsp paprika
Sprigs of parsley, to garnish
New potatoes and peas, to serve

① Put the plaice fillets in a frying pan (skillet) and pour over a little of the milk. Season lightly with salt and pepper. Bring to the boil, reduce the heat, cover and simmer gently for 10–15 minutes, until the fish flakes. Lift out the fish with a slotted spoon and reserve the milk.

② Meanwhile, melt the margarine or spread in a pan, add the mushrooms and cook gently for 4–5 minutes until soft.

③ Stir in the flour and paprika and cook for 1 further minute. Gradually add the remaining milk, together with the reserved milk left from cooking the fish. Bring to the boil, stirring all the time. Season with a little salt and pepper.

④ Arrange the fish on a warm serving plate, pour over the sauce and garnish with sprigs of parsley. Serve with new potatoes and peas.

### PREPARATION AND COOKING TIME: 20 MINUTES

# Baked salmon steaks
## SERVES 4

4 salmon steaks
25 g/1 oz/2 tbsp sunflower margarine or low-fat spread
4 bay leaves
4 sprigs of parsley
1 onion, quartered
1 lemon, cut into 4 wedges
Salt and freshly ground black pepper
New potatoes, baby sweetcorn (corn) and mangetout
  (snow peas), to serve

① Preheat the oven to 180°C/350°F/gas mark 4.

② Place each salmon steak on a square of foil large enough to make a parcel. Put a knob of margarine or spread on each steak, and top with a bay leaf, a parsley sprig, a piece of onion and a slice of lemon. Season with a little salt and freshly ground pepper.

③ Wrap the foil to make little parcels and put them in an ovenproof dish. Add enough water to cover the bottom of the dish. Bake in the preheated oven for 15–20 minutes, until the flesh flakes.

④ Serve with new potatoes, baby sweetcorn and mangetout.

PREPARATION AND COOKING TIME: 20 MINUTES

# Smoked haddock with sweetcorn
## SERVES 4

550 g/1¼ lb undyed smoked haddock fillet
25 g/1 oz/2 tbsp sunflower margarine or low-fat spread
25 g/1 oz/¼ cup plain (all-purpose) flour
150 ml/¼ pt/⅔ cup semi-skimmed milk
Salt and freshly ground black pepper
320 g/12 oz/1 medium can of sweetcorn (corn), drained
60 ml/4 tbsp low-fat crème fraîche
Sprigs of parsley, to garnish
New potatoes, to serve

① Preheat the oven to 180°C/350°F/gas mark 4.

② Place the haddock in a large frying pan (skillet) and add just enough boiling water to cover. Simmer for 5 minutes. Remove the fish, cut into pieces and place in a casserole (Dutch oven). Lift out the fish with a slotted spoon and reserve 150 ml/¼ pt/⅔ cup of the cooking liquid.

③ Melt the margarine or spread in a saucepan and stir in the flour. Cook, stirring, for 1 minute, then gradually add the milk and the reserved cooking liquid. Bring to the boil, stirring continuously. Season with a little salt and pepper.

④ Stir in the sweetcorn and pour the sauce over the haddock. Cover and cook in the preheated oven for 20 minutes.

⑤ Just before serving, stir in the crème fraîche. Garnish with sprigs of parsley and serve with new potatoes.

PREPARATION AND COOKING TIME: 30 MINUTES

# fish and mushroom pie
## SERVES 4

450 g/1 lb potatoes
50 g/2 oz/½ cup sunflower margarine or low-fat spread
150 g/¼ pt/⅔ cup semi-skimmed milk
550 g/1¼ lb white fish such as cod or haddock
25 g/1 oz/¼ cup plain (all-purpose) flour
100 g/4 oz mushrooms, sliced
Salt and freshly ground black pepper
25 g/1 oz/¼ cup reduced-fat Cheddar cheese
Green vegetables, to serve

① Preheat the oven to 190°C/375°F/gas mark 5.

② Cook the potatoes in plenty of boiling, lightly salted water for 15–20 minutes, until soft. Drain, add a knob of the margarine or spread and a little of the milk. Mash to a smooth consistency.

③ Meanwhile, put the fish in a saucepan, cover with water and cook gently for 6–7 minutes, until the fish flakes. Drain and reserve the cooking liquid.

④ Melt the remaining margarine or spread in another pan and gently fry (sauté) the mushrooms for 3–4 minutes, until soft. Stir in the flour and cook for 1 minute. Gradually add the rest of the milk and 150 ml/¼ pt of the reserved fish stock. Bring to the boil, stirring continuously, and cook until the sauce is thick and smooth. Add the flaked fish and season with a little salt and pepper. Turn the mixture into an ovenproof dish.

⑤ Cover with sliced tomatoes, then spoon over the mashed potato. Sprinkle over the cheese. Bake for 30 minutes, until the top is golden brown.

⑥ Serve hot with green vegetables.

PREPARATION AND COOKING TIME: 50 MINUTES

# Smoked haddock cassoulet
## SERVES 4

450 g/1 lb smoked haddock
225 g/8 oz monkfish tail
1 bay leaf
Salt and freshly ground black pepper
30 ml/2 tbsp vegetable or sunflower oil
1 onion, chopped
1 celery stick, chopped
1 carrot, chopped
1 garlic clove, crushed
100 g/4 oz lean bacon rashers (slices), chopped
50 ml/2 fl oz/¼ cup dry white wine
425 g/15 oz/1 large can of cannellini beans, drained
10 ml/2 tsp dried mixed herbs
4 tomatoes, skinned and quartered
Wholemeal or multi-grain bread, to serve

① Preheat the oven to 190°C/375°F/gas mark 5.

② Put the fish into a large pan of water. Add the bay leaf and a pinch of salt and pepper. Bring to the boil, then reduce the heat and simmer for 10–12 minutes, until the flesh just flakes. Drain, reserving 600 ml/1 pt/2½ cups of the liquid. Skin, bone and flake the fish and set aside.

③ Heat the oil in a frying pan (skillet), add the onion, celery, carrot and garlic and cook gently for 5 minutes. Add the bacon and cook for a further 3 minutes.

④ Pour in the reserved fish stock and the wine. Add the beans and herbs. Cook briskly for 10 minutes, until the liquid has reduced and the mixture is very thick.

⑤ Add the flaked fish and the tomatoes. Check the seasoning, then transfer the mixture to a shallow casserole and bake in the preheated oven for 30 minutes.

⑥ Serve hot with wholemeal or multi-grain bread.

PREPARATION AND COOKING TIME: 1 HOUR

# *Monkfish in black bean sauce*
## SERVES 4

*Monkfish can be rather bland on its own, so here's how to pep it up with a tasty sauce. Jars of black bean sauce are available in most supermarkets.*

---

**450 g/1 lb monkfish**
**Salt and freshly ground black pepper**
**450 g/1 lb spinach**
**60 ml/4 tbsp sunflower or vegetable oil**
**4 garlic cloves, crushed**
**10 ml/2 tsp grated fresh root ginger**
**15 ml/1 tbsp soy sauce**
**30 ml/2 tbsp vegetable or chicken stock**
**4–5 spring onions (scallions), chopped**
**1 green (bell) pepper, sliced**
**60 ml/4 tbsp black bean sauce**
**Plain boiled rice or noodles, to serve**

---

① Cut the fish into large chunks and put into a bowl. Sprinkle with 2.5 ml/½ tsp salt and some pepper and leave to stand for 20 minutes.

② Remove the stalks from the spinach and tear the leaves into pieces. Wash thoroughly in cold water and shake dry.

③ Heat half the oil in a wok or large frying pan (skillet). When hot, add half the garlic and half the ginger and stir-fry for 1 minute. Add the spinach and stir-fry for a further 2 minutes. Add the soy sauce and stock and continue cooking for 1–2 minutes until the liquid has evaporated. Transfer to a warmed serving dish.

④ Add the remaining oil to the wok or frying pan and gently stir-fry the fish for about 2 minutes, until browned. Drain on kitchen paper (paper towels).

⑤ Add the remaining garlic and ginger, spring onions and green pepper to the pan. Stir-fry for 1 minute, then add the black bean sauce. Heat through, then add the fish and cook for a further minute.

⑥ Spoon the fish into a warmed dish and serve with the stir-fried spinach and boiled rice or noodles.

PREPARATION AND COOKING TIME: 10–15 MINUTES PLUS STANDING

# Seafood stir-fry
## SERVES 4

45 ml/3 tbsp groundnut oil
1 cos or iceberg lettuce, shredded
2 celery sticks, cut into matchsticks
1 carrot, cut into matchsticks
1 garlic clove, crushed
350 g/12 oz cod or haddock fillet,
  cut into 2.5 cm/1 in chunks
100 g/4 oz cooked peeled prawns (shrimp)
410 g/14 oz/1 large can of baby sweetcorn (corn),
  drained
5 ml/1 tsp anchovy essence (extract)
Salt and freshly ground black pepper
Plain boiled rice or noodles, to serve

① Heat 15 ml/1 tbsp of the oil in a wok or large frying pan (skillet) until smoking. Add the lettuce and fry (sauté) for 30 seconds. Transfer to a serving dish and keep warm.

② Heat the remaining oil in the pan until smoking. Add the celery, carrot, garlic and fish. Stir-fry over a high heat for 2–3 minutes.

③ Lower the heat and add the prawns, baby sweetcorn and anchovy essence. Toss well together and heat through for 2–3 minutes.

④ Season to taste with a little salt and pepper. Spoon on top of the lettuce and serve with plain rice or noodles.

PREPARATION AND COOKING TIME: 15–20 MINUTES

# Spicy cod and beans
## SERVES 4

*Make this fish dish as spicy as you like by adjusting the amount of chilli powder. The butter (lima) beans add valuable fibre.*

---

30 ml/2 tbsp sunflower or vegetable oil
2 celery sticks, finely chopped
2 onions, finely chopped
2 garlic cloves, crushed
4 tomatoes, chopped
425 g/15 oz/1 large can of butter beans
2.5 ml/½ tsp chilli powder
120 ml/4 fl oz/½ cup dry white wine
550 g/1¼ lb cod fillet
30 ml/2 tbsp chopped fresh parsley
Freshly ground black pepper
Brown rice, to serve

---

① Heat the oil in a pan and add the celery, onion and garlic. Cook for 5 minutes. Add the tomatoes, beans and chilli powder. Simmer, uncovered, for 10 minutes.

② Meanwhile, heat the wine in a pan, add the fish and poach gently for 4–5 minutes, or until just cooked through.

③ Remove the skin from the cooked fish, cut it into chunks and add, together with the cooking liquid, to the tomato and bean mixture. Add the parsley and season with plenty of pepper.

④ Serve with brown rice.

PREPARATION AND COOKING TIME: 15 MINUTES

## Spanish chicken
### SERVES 4

hicken joints, skinned and trimmed
g/1 oz/¼ cup plain (all-purpose) flour
t and freshly ground black pepper
ml/2 tbsp olive oil
nion, finely chopped
garlic cloves, crushed
ed (bell) pepper, seeded and chopped
green pepper, seeded and chopped
5 ml/8 fl oz/1 cup chicken stock
0 g/6 oz mushrooms, sliced
tomatoes, sliced
2 black olives, stoned (pitted)
ain boiled rice, new potatoes or pasta, to serve

1. Preheat the oven to 160°C/325°F/gas mark 3.

2. Pat the chicken dry with kitchen paper (paper towels).

3. Sprinkle the flour on to a plate and season with a little salt and pepper. Roll the chicken pieces in the flour until they are well coated.

4. Heat half the olive oil in a large frying pan (skillet). Add the chicken pieces and fry (sauté) them for 5–7 minutes on each side, or until they are lightly browned. Transfer to a large ovenproof casserole dish (Dutch oven).

5. Add the onion, garlic and peppers to the pan and fry for 5 minutes, stirring continuously. Spoon the vegetables over the chicken pieces in the casserole. Pour over the stock. Cover the casserole and cook in the preheated oven for about 1 hour, until the chicken is tender.

6. Heat the remaining olive oil in a small frying pan and cook the mushrooms and tomatoes over a moderate heat for 5 minutes. Add to the casserole with the black olives and cook for 5 minutes. Serve hot with plain rice, new potatoes or pasta.

PREPARATION AND COOKING TIME: 1 HOUR 30 MINUTES

---

## Poultry main courses

Most of the fat in poultry is contained in the skin, so it is a good idea to remove this before cooking. Chicken and turkey are endlessly versatile: they can be roasted, grilled (broiled), casseroled or stir-fried and can take on any flavour and cooking style, from Mediterranean to spicy Indian, and they are also inexpensive, which makes them ideal for midweek suppers. For that special occasion, I have included a deceptively simple but really delicious recipe for casseroled pheasant.

Many of the recipes already contain carbohydrate – potatoes, rice or noodles – or I have suggested what goes well as an accompaniment. These are suggestions only – choose whatever suits your own family's tastes. And remember: you can never eat too many vegetables.

# Roast chicken and vegetables with rosemary
### SERVES 4

*Sweet potatoes and fennel are particularly delicious roasted in a little olive oil. Other unusual vegetables that are good to try are butternut squash and mooli.*

350 g/12 oz potatoes, quartered
4 chicken joints, skinned
60 ml/4 tbsp olive oil
30 ml/2 tbsp chopped fresh rosemary
225 g/8 oz sweet potatoes, cubed
225 g/8 oz parsnips, sliced
1 fennel bulb, quartered
1 onion, chopped
Salt and freshly ground black pepper
Peas or French (green) beans, to serve

① Preheat the oven to 190°C/375°F/gas mark 5.

② Put the potatoes into a saucepan of lightly salted water, bring to the boil and cook for 5 minutes. Drain.

③ Put the chicken joints in a ovenproof dish. Brush with a little olive oil and sprinkle over half the chopped rosemary.

④ Put the parboiled potatoes, sweet potatoes, parsnips, fennel and onion into another ovenproof dish. Pour over the remaining olive oil and toss so that the vegetables are well coated. Sprinkle with the remaining rosemary and season with a little salt and pepper.

⑤ Put both dishes into the preheated oven and cook for about 1 hour, until the chicken is tender and the vegetables crisp and browned.

⑥ Serve with peas or French beans.

PREPARATION AND COOKING TIME: 1 HOUR 15 MINUTES

# Chicken with spring veget
### SERVES 4

*Try this dish in the spring, when the peas an young and sweet, and serve it with early ne*

30 ml/2 tbsp vegetable or sunflower oil
4 chicken joints, skinned
225 g/8 oz shallots
120 ml/4 fl oz/½ cup chicken stock
60 ml/4 tbsp dry white wine
1 tomato, peeled and sliced
Salt and freshly ground black pepper
120 ml/4 fl oz/½ cup water
175 g/6 oz/1½ cups shelled fresh or frozen pea
100 g/4 oz baby carrots, sliced
175 g/6 oz spring (collard) greens
2 sprigs of thyme
New potatoes, to serve

① Heat the oil in a large frying pan (skillet) and f the chicken joints for 3–4 minutes on each side, are golden brown. Cover and continue cooking ge further 3–4 minutes. Remove the chicken with spoon and set aside.

② Finely chop one of the shallots and add to the pan the stock and wine, and add the tomato. Stir well a for 5 minutes. Season to taste with a little salt and

③ Return the chicken to the pan, cover and sim 20 minutes.

④ Meanwhile, bring the water to the boil in a saucep add the peas, carrots, spring greens and sprigs of t Cover and simmer gently for about 5 minutes, un vegetables are tender.

⑤ Drain the vegetables and add to the chicken. Heat th gently for 2 minutes.

⑥ Serve with new potatoes.

PREPARATION AND COOKING TIME: 40 MINUTES

# Creamy Mediterranean chicken

## SERVES 4

15 ml/1 tbsp olive oil
4 chicken breasts, boned and skinned
100 g/4 oz shallots, halved
1 garlic clove, crushed
1 red (bell) pepper, chopped
1 green pepper, chopped
100 g/4 oz button mushrooms
120 ml/4 fl oz/½ cup chicken stock
60 ml/4 tbsp dry white wine
25 g/1 oz/¼ cup cornflour (cornstarch)
15 ml/1 tbsp chopped fresh basil
15 ml/1 tbsp chopped fresh marjoram
5 ml/1 tsp Dijon mustard
200 ml/7 fl oz/scant 1 cup crème fraîche
Freshly ground black pepper
100 g/4 oz stoned (pitted) black olives
Plain boiled rice and a green salad, to serve

① Heat the oil in a large pan and fry (sauté) the chicken breasts over a high heat for 2 minutes on each side, until browned.

② Reduce the heat, add the shallots and garlic and cook gently for 3–4 minutes, until softened.

③ Add the peppers and mushrooms and continue cooking for 3–4 minutes.

④ Stir in the stock and wine, bring to the boil, cover and simmer for about 15 minutes, until the chicken is tender.

⑤ Mix the cornflour to a thin paste with a little water. Stir into the pan and bring to the boil, stirring until the sauce is thickened.

⑥ Reduce the heat, add the remaining ingredients and gently heat through.

⑦ Serve with plain rice and a green salad.

PREPARATION AND COOKING TIME: 30 MINUTES

# Chicken pilaf
SERVES 4

---

225 g/8 oz/1 cup brown rice
900 ml/1½ pts/3¾ cups chicken stock
75 g/3 oz/½ cup raisins
225 ml/8 fl oz/1 cup fresh unsweetened orange juice
45 ml/3 tbsp groundnut or vegetable oil
1 onion, chopped
2.5 ml/½ tsp ground ginger
8 chicken drumsticks, skinned
50 g/2 oz/½ cup pine nuts
30 ml/2 tbsp chopped fresh mint, to garnish

---

① Preheat the oven to 180°C/350°F/gas mark 4.

② Put the rice into a large casserole (Dutch oven) and stir in 750 ml/1¼ pts/3 cups of the stock. Cover and place in the oven for 15 minutes.

③ Meanwhile, put the raisins in a small bowl and pour over the orange juice. Set aside.

④ Heat the oil in a large frying pan (skillet), add the onion and ginger and fry (sauté) for 1 minute.

⑤ Add the chicken drumsticks and fry for 3–4 minutes on each side until browned all over. Remove the chicken and set aside.

⑥ Pour off any surplus fat in the pan. Add the remaining stock and bring to a boil.

⑦ Remove the casserole from the oven and stir the onion and stock mixture into the rice. Add the raisins and orange juice and the pine nuts. Add the chicken. Cover and return to the oven for a further 30 minutes.

⑧ Serve garnished with chopped mint.

PREPARATION AND COOKING TIME: 50 MINUTES

## *Chicken chow mein*
### SERVES 4

4 chicken breasts, skinned and boned
350 g/12 oz egg noodles
30 ml/2 tbsp cooking oil
1 onion, sliced
2 garlic cloves, sliced
2 carrots, grated
450 g/1 lb beansprouts
30 ml/2 tbsp light soy sauce
15 ml/1 tbsp sesame oil

① Slice the chicken into thin strips.

② Put the noodles into a large saucepan of boiling water and cook for 4 minutes, or according to the instructions on the packet. Drain and reserve.

③ Meanwhile, heat the oil in a wok or large frying pan (skillet), add the chicken and stir-fry for 2–3 minutes, until the chicken is white.

④ Add the onion, garlic and carrot, and stir-fry for another 2 minutes.

⑤ Add the beansprouts, soy sauce, sesame oil and noodles.

⑥ Mix everything together thoroughly and heat gently for a few minutes before serving.

PREPARATION AND COOKING TIME: 15 MINUTES

# Chicken biryani

SERVES 4

275 g/10 oz/1¼ cups basmati rice
1 cinnamon stick
3 cloves
10 cardamom pods
2.5 ml/½ tsp saffron strands or powder
10 ml/2 tsp hot milk
45 ml/3 tbsp sunflower or vegetable oil
3 onions, sliced
4 chicken breasts, skinned, boned and cubed
5 ml/1 tsp ground coriander
5 ml/1 tsp ground cumin
2.5 ml/½ tsp chilli powder
3 garlic cloves, crushed
5 ml/1 tsp grated fresh root ginger
Juice of 1 lemon
4 tomatoes, sliced
30 ml/2 tbsp chopped fresh coriander (cilantro)
150 ml/¼ pt/⅔ cup plain low-fat yoghurt
150 ml/¼ pt/⅔ cup water
25 g/1 oz/⅙ cup flaked (slivered) almonds, toasted, and
   sprigs of coriander, to garnish

① Preheat the oven to 190°C/375°F/gas mark 5.

② Bring a pan of lightly salted water to the boil. Add the rice, cinnamon stick, cloves and half the cardamom pods. Boil for 2 minutes, then drain and set aside, leaving the spices in the rice.

③ Remove the seeds from the remaining cardamom pods and bruise them lightly.

④ Put the saffron into the hot milk to soak.

⑤ Heat the oil in a frying pan (skillet) and fry the onions for 5 minutes, until lightly browned. Add the chicken, ground spices, cardamom, garlic, ginger and lemon juice. Continue cooking for 5 minutes, stirring continuously.

⑥ Tip the mixture into a casserole dish (Dutch oven). Arrange the tomato slices on top and sprinkle with coriander. Spoon over the yoghurt and top with the rice.

⑦ Drizzle the saffron liquid over the rice and add the water. Cover the casserole dish tightly and cook in the preheated oven for 1 hour.

⑧ Remove the whole spices and serve at once, garnished with flaked almonds and sprigs of coriander.

PREPARATION AND COOKING TIME: 1 HOUR 15 MINUTES

# Stir-fried chicken and peppers
SERVES 4

---

30 ml/2 tbsp sunflower or vegetable oil
15 ml/1 tbsp sesame oil
4 chicken breasts, cut into bite-sized pieces
1 red (bell) pepper, diced
1 green pepper, diced
1 yellow pepper, diced
6 spring onions (scallions), chopped
2 garlic cloves, sliced
30 ml/2 tbsp light soy sauce
Plain boiled rice or noodles, to serve

---

① Heat the oils in a wok or large frying pan (skillet). When the pan is really hot, add the chicken and stir-fry for 4–5 minutes, until the flesh is white.

② Turn down the heat to moderate. Push the chicken to one side of the pan and put the peppers, onions and garlic on the other side. Continue cooking for 3–4 minutes, then mix the chicken and peppers together and add the soy sauce.

③ Heat through for another couple of minutes.

④ Serve with plain rice or noodles.

PREPARATION AND COOKING TIME: 15 MINUTES

# Thai chicken with noodles
## SERVES 4

4 chicken breasts, skinned and boned
Grated rind and juice of 2 limes
15 ml/1 tbsp sunflower or vegetable oil
2 garlic cloves, thinly sliced
350 g/12 oz egg noodles
½ cucumber, peeled and sliced
6 spring onions (scallions), sliced
30 ml/2 tbsp chopped fresh coriander (cilantro)
2.5 ml/½ tsp chilli powder
5 ml/1 tsp clear honey

① Place the chicken in a non-metallic dish. Spoon over half the lime rind and juice and leave to marinate for 30 minutes.

② Heat the oil in a pan, add the chicken and garlic and fry (sauté) for 6–7 minutes, until the chicken is completely cooked through.

③ Meanwhile, cook the noodles in a large saucepan of boiling, salted water for 4 minutes, or according to the packet instructions. Drain and rinse under cold, running water.

④ Mix together the cucumber, spring onions, coriander, chilli and noodles.

⑤ Mix the remaining lime juice and rind with the honey, and stir into the noodles. Spoon on to a serving plate.

⑥ Slice the cooked chicken and arrange on top of the noodles.

PREPARATION AND COOKING TIME: 15 MINUTES PLUS MARINATING

# Braised turkey with mushrooms
### SERVES 6

---

30 ml/2 tbsp vegetable or sunflower oil
1 onion, sliced
2 garlic cloves, crushed
900 g/2 lb rolled turkey breast
2.5 ml/½ tsp grated nutmeg
Freshly ground black pepper
225 g/8 oz button mushrooms, halved
300 ml/½ pt/1¼ cups chicken stock
5 ml/1 tsp dried mixed herbs
15 g/½ oz/2 tbsp cornflour (cornstarch)
New potatoes, peas and carrots, to serve

---

① Preheat the oven to 180°C/350°F/gas mark 4.

② Heat the oil in a casserole dish (Dutch oven), add the onion and garlic and cook gently for 2–3 minutes, until soft.

③ Add the rolled turkey breast and sprinkle it with nutmeg and pepper.

④ Add the mushrooms, stock and herbs. Cover and cook in the oven for about 1 hour, or until the turkey is tender.

⑤ Remove the turkey from the casserole, carve into slices and arrange on a heated serving dish. Spoon the mushrooms over the turkey.

⑥ Put the casserole with the stock back on top of the stove. Mix the cornflour to a thin paste with a little water. Stir into the stock and bring to the boil, stirring until the sauce thickens. Pour over the chicken and mushrooms.

⑦ Serve with new potatoes, peas and carrots.

PREPARATION AND COOKING TIME: 1 HOUR 10 MINUTES

# Spicy turkey and beans
## SERVES 4

*This is a good recipe for finishing up cold, leftover turkey, using storecupboard ingredients. Adjust the quantity of chilli powder, according to how hot you like it.*

25 g/1 oz/2 tbsp sunflower margarine or low-fat spread
2 onions, chopped
15 g/½ oz/2 tbsp plain (all-purpose) flour
2.5 ml/½ tsp chilli powder
400 g/14 oz/1 large can of tomatoes
30 ml/2 tbsp tomato purée (paste)
15 ml/1 tbsp Worcestershire sauce
300 ml/½ pt/1¼ cups chicken stock
Freshly ground black pepper
450 g/1 lb/4 cups diced cooked turkey
200 g/7 oz/1 small can of pimientos, drained and
  chopped
425 g/15 oz/1 large can of red kidney beans, drained
Brown rice, to serve

① Melt the margarine or spread in a large saucepan and gently cook the onions for 3–4 minutes, until softened but not browned.

② Stir in the flour and chilli powder. Cook for 1 minute, then stir in the tomatoes, tomato purée, Worcestershire sauce and stock. Season with pepper. Bring to the boil, reduce the heat, then cover and simmer for 30 minutes.

③ Stir in the cooked turkey with the pimientos and beans. Simmer for 10 minutes. Serve with brown rice.

PREPARATION AND COOKING TIME: 45 MINUTES

# ℘heasant in red wine

### SERVES 4

30 ml/2 tbsp sunflower or vegetable oil
1 pheasant
2 onions, finely chopped
1 clove of garlic, crushed
1 carrot, sliced
2 celery sticks, sliced
15 ml/1 tbsp chopped fresh thyme
1 bay leaf
150 ml/¼ pt/⅔ cup red wine
150 ml/¼ pt/⅔ cup chicken stock
Freshly ground black pepper
15 g/½ oz/1 tbsp butter
15 g/½ oz/2 tbsp plain (all-purpose) flour
New potatoes and French (green) beans, to serve

① Heat the oil in a frying pan (skillet) and fry (sauté) the whole pheasant, turning it to brown all sides. Transfer to a large flameproof casserole (Dutch oven).

② Put the onions, garlic, carrot and celery into the frying pan and cook for 4–5 minutes until soft. Transfer to the casserole.

③ Add the thyme, bay leaf, red wine and stock to the frying pan. Stir and season with plenty of freshly ground pepper. Pour into the casserole.

④ Set the casserole over a high heat and bring to the boil. Turn down the heat, cover and simmer for 1 hour, until the pheasant is tender.

⑤ Transfer the pheasant to a warm serving dish. Skim any fat from the liquid in the casserole and remove the bay leaf. Heat briskly, until the sauce has reduced by half.

⑥ Cream the butter and flour together and whisk into the sauce to thicken it. Pour over the pheasant in the serving dish.

⑦ Serve with new potatoes and French beans.

PREPARATION AND COOKING TIME: 1 HOUR 15 MINUTES

# Meat main courses

**R**ed meat can be high in saturated fat, so always choose meat that is lean and cut off any surplus fat. You can reduce the amount of meat you eat and add valuable fibre by choosing stir-fried dishes that contain lots of vegetables as well as meat, or by replacing some of the meat with pulses, as I have done in some of these recipes.

# Cottage pie
## SERVES 4

700 g/1½ lb potatoes, quartered
25 g/1 oz/¼ cup sunflower margarine or low-fat spread,
    plus extra for topping
A little semi-skimmed milk
15 ml/1 tbsp sunflower or vegetable oil
1 onion, chopped
2 carrots, chopped
350 g/12 oz extra-lean minced (ground) beef
100 g/4 oz/⅔ cup red lentils
25 g/1 oz/¼ cup plain (all-purpose) flour
175 ml/6 fl oz/¾ cup beef stock
30 ml/2 tbsp tomato purée (paste)
Salt and freshly ground black pepper
Green vegetables, to serve

①  Preheat the oven to 190°C/375°F/gas mark 5.

②  Cook the potatoes in plenty of boiling, lightly salted water
    for about 20 minutes, until really soft. Drain and mash with
    the margarine or spread and enough milk to give a smooth
    creamy consistency.

③  Heat the oil in a pan and gently fry (sauté) the onion and
    carrots for 4–5 minutes, until softened. Add the meat and
    cook until browned, stirring occasionally. Add the lentils.

④  Sprinkle with the flour and cook for 1 minute, stirring, then
    add the stock and tomato purée. Season with salt and
    pepper, bring to the boil, then reduce the heat, cover and
    simmer for 20 minutes.

⑤  Spoon the meat mixture into an ovenproof dish and spread
    the mashed potato on top. Decorate the surface using a
    fork and dot with a little margarine or low-fat spread.

⑥  Cook in the preheated oven for 30 minutes.

⑦  Serve with green vegetables.

PREPARATION AND COOKING TIME: 1 HOUR

# Italian-style meatballs
### SERVES 4

350 g/12 oz extra-lean minced (ground) beef
100 g/4 oz/⅔ cup red lentils
1 onion, finely chopped
Salt and freshly ground pepper
2 slices of bread
15–30 ml/1–2 tbsp semi-skimmed milk
1 egg, beaten
A little flour
50 g/2 oz/½ cup sunflower margarine or low-fat spread
450 ml/¾ pt/2 cups beef stock
10 ml/2 tsp tomato purée (paste)
15 g/½ oz/2 tbsp cornflour (cornstarch)
5 ml/1 tsp vinegar
15 ml/1 tbsp chopped fresh parsley
Mashed potatoes and broccoli, or pasta and green salad,
    to serve

① Put the minced beef, lentils and onion into a bowl and season with salt and pepper.

② Trim the crusts from the bread and place in a small bowl. Add the milk and allow the bread to soak for a few minutes, then squeeze away any excess moisture.

③ Add the bread and the egg to the meat. Mix the ingredients until well-blended – this is best done with lightly oiled fingers. Shape the mixture into 12 small balls and roll in flour with a little salt and pepper added.

④ Melt the margarine or spread in a frying pan (skillet) and fry (sauté) the meatballs until browned on all sides – shake the pan gently from time to time so that they keep a nice round shape. Lift the meatballs from the frying pan with a slotted spoon and place in a flameproof casserole (Dutch oven).

⑤ Pour away any fat remaining in the frying pan and add the stock and tomato purée to the hot pan. Stir to mix well and bring to the boil. Pour over the meatballs. Cover the casserole and simmer gently for 45–50 minutes.

⑥ Blend the cornflour to a thin paste with a little water and stir into the casserole. Check the seasoning, then add the vinegar to sharpen the flavour to taste.

⑦ Sprinkle with chopped parsley and serve with either mashed potatoes and broccoli, or pasta and a green salad.

PREPARATION AND COOKING TIME: 1 HOUR 10 MINUTES

# Chilli con carne
### SERVES 4

30 ml/2 tbsp sunflower or vegetable oil
1 large onion, sliced
1 garlic clove, crushed
1 green (bell) pepper, sliced
350 g/12 oz extra-lean minced (ground) beef
5 ml/1 tsp chilli powder
5 ml/1 tsp ground cumin
400 g/14 oz/1 large can of tomatoes
15 ml/1 tbsp tomato purée (paste)
425 g/15 oz/1 large can of red kidney beans, drained
Salt and freshly ground black pepper
Plain rice, baked potatoes or taco shells and green salad,
    to serve

① Heat the oil and gently cook the onion, garlic and green pepper for 4–5 minutes, until softened.

② Add the meat and cook until browned, stirring frequently.

③ Stir in the rest of the ingredients, and season with a little salt and pepper. Bring to the boil, then reduce the heat, cover and cook gently for 45–50 minutes.

④ Serve with plain rice, baked potatoes or taco shells and a green salad.

PREPARATION AND COOKING TIME: 1 HOUR

# Beef in oyster sauce with stir-fried cabbage
## SERVES 4

225 g/8 oz rump or fillet steak
30 ml/2 tbsp dry sherry
30 ml/2 tbsp soy sauce
75 ml/5 tbsp sunflower or vegetable oil
25 g/1 oz/¼ cup cornflour (cornstarch)
15 ml/1 tbsp water
4–6 spring onions (scallions)
15 ml/1 tbsp grated fresh root ginger
30 ml/2 tbsp oyster sauce
350 g/12 oz egg noodles
2 garlic cloves
1 cabbage
45 ml/3 tbsp beef stock

① Cut the steak into thin strips and put into a small bowl with the sherry, 15 ml/1 tbsp of the soy sauce and 15 ml/1 tbsp of the oil. Mix the cornflour with the water and add.

② Heat 30 ml/2 tbsp of the remaining oil in a wok or large frying pan (skillet). When it is very hot, add the beef and stir-fry for 3 minutes.

③ Add the spring onions, half the ginger and the oyster sauce and continue stir-frying for a further 2 minutes. Turn into a warm serving dish.

④ Cook the noodles in a large pan of boiling, lightly salted water for 4–5 minutes, or according to the instructions.

⑤ Wipe clean the wok or frying pan with kitchen paper (paper towels) and heat the remaining oil. When hot, add the garlic and remaining ginger and stir-fry for 1 minute.

⑥ Add the cabbage and stir-fry for 3 minutes, then add the remaining soy sauce and stock and heat through. Turn into a serving dish.

⑦ Drain the noodles and serve with the beef and cabbage.

PREPARATION AND COOKING TIME: 15 MINUTES

# Lamb steaks with flageolet beans
## SERVES 4

*Flageolet beans are kidney-shaped and pale green in colour.*
*They go particularly well with lamb.*

30 ml/2 tbsp olive oil
5 lean lamb steaks
10 ml/2 tsp chopped fresh rosemary
2 garlic cloves, crushed
425 g/15 oz/1 large can of flageolet beans, drained
100 g/4 oz button (pearl) onions
50 ml/2 fl oz/¼ cup dry white wine
300 ml/½ pt/1¼ cups chicken or vegetable stock
Salt and freshly ground black pepper
Chopped fresh parsley, to garnish
Wholemeal or multi-grain bread and tomato salad,
    to serve

① Heat the oil in a frying pan (skillet), add the lamb steaks and cook for 8–10 minutes on each side until tender and browned. Sprinkle with the rosemary, remove to a serving dish and keep warm.

② Add the garlic, beans and onions to the pan and cook gently for 5 minutes.

③ Pour in the wine and cook until reduced a little, then stir in the stock. Season with a little salt and pepper and simmer for 10 minutes.

④ Spoon the beans around the lamb steaks, sprinkle with chopped parsley and serve with wholemeal or multi-grain bread and a tomato salad.

PREPARATION AND COOKING TIME: 35 MINUTES

# Oriental lamb

SERVES 4

*This lamb stew includes potatoes, so there is plenty of carbohydrate, but you may wish to serve it with peas or beans for added fibre.*

**30 ml/2 tbsp sunflower or vegetable oil**
**25 g/1 oz/¼ cup sunflower margarine or low-fat spread**
**450 g/1 lb lean lamb, cubed**
**450 g/1 lb baby new potatoes**
**225 g/8 oz small pickling onions, skinned**
**25 g/1 oz/¼ cup plain (all-purpose) flour**
**5 ml/1 tsp ground ginger**
**300 ml/½ pt/1¼ cups vegetable or chicken stock**
**45 ml/3 tbsp soy sauce**
**Freshly ground black pepper**
**2 canned pimientos, chopped**
**Peas or French (green) beans, to serve**

① Heat the oil and margarine or spread in a large pan. Add the meat and fry (sauté) for 4–5 minutes, until browned. Remove from the pan with a slotted spoon.

② Add the potatoes and onions to the pan and fry (sauté) for 4–5 minutes, until lightly browned, turning frequently.

③ Return the meat to the pan, sprinkle in the flour and ginger and stir well. Cook gently, stirring, for 2 minutes.

④ Add the stock and soy sauce, and plenty of pepper. Bring to the boil, then cover and simmer for 30 minutes, or until the meat is tender.

⑤ Add the chopped pimientos. Serve accompanied with peas or French beans.

PREPARATION AND COOKING TIME: 40 MINUTES

# Lamb shanks with rosemary in red wine
## SERVES 4

*Lamb shanks need to be cooked slowly for a long time to make them meltingly tender. This dish tastes even better if you make it in advance and then reheat it thoroughly.*

45 ml/3 tbsp sunflower oil
A little flour
Salt and freshly ground black pepper
4 lamb shanks, about 1.25 kg/2½ lb in all
1 onion, chopped
2 garlic cloves, crushed
300 ml/½ pt/1¼ cups chicken or vegetable stock
150 ml/¼ pt/⅔ cup red wine
45 ml/3 tbsp chopped fresh rosemary
New potatoes and green vegetables, to serve

① Heat the oil in a large, heavy-bottomed saucepan.

② Season the flour with a little salt and pepper. Dust the lamb shanks with this mixture and brown in the hot oil.

③ Turn down the heat a little, add the onion and garlic and cook for 2–3 minutes.

④ Add the stock, wine, rosemary, a little salt and plenty of black pepper.

⑤ Bring to the boil, then reduce the heat, cover and simmer on a very low heat for 2–2½ hours, until the lamb is tender and falling away from the bone.

⑥ Serve with new potatoes and green vegetables.

PREPARATION AND COOKING TIME: 2¼–2¾ HOURS

# Stir-fried lambs' liver and vegetables
## SERVES 4

*Liver becomes hard and dry if it is cooked for too long, so keep the stir-frying stage short.*

450 g/1 lb lambs' liver
30 ml/2 tbsp dry sherry
Salt and freshly ground black pepper
30 ml/2 tbsp sunflower or vegetable oil
2 onions, finely sliced
1.5 ml/¼ tsp ground ginger
3 tomatoes, thinly sliced
150 ml/¼ pt/⅔ cup vegetable or chicken stock
350 g/12 oz egg noodles
*For the vegetables:*
15 ml/1 tbsp sunflower or vegetable oil
15 ml/1 tbsp sesame oil
5–6 spring onions, sliced
5 ml/1 tsp grated fresh root ginger
2 carrots, cut into thin sticks
350 ml/12 oz beansprouts
30 ml/2 tbsp soy sauce

① Using a very sharp knife, cut the liver into wafer-thin strips. Place in a shallow bowl and spoon over the sherry. Season with a little salt and pepper. Cover and leave to marinate for 2–3 hours.

② Heat the oil in a large frying pan (skillet). When very hot, add the liver strips and stir-fry briskly for 1–2 minutes, until browned. Remove from the pan with a slotted spoon and keep warm.

③ Add the onions and ginger to the pan and cook for 3 minutes, then add the tomatoes and continue cooking for another 2 minutes. Add the stock and check the seasoning. Bring just to the boil, then pour over the liver.

④ Cook the noodles in a large pan of boiling water for 4–5 minutes, or according to the instructions on the packet. Drain.

⑤ While the noodles are cooking, rinse out the frying pan and heat the oils for stir-frying the vegetables. Stir-fry over a high heat for 3–4 minutes. Add the soy sauce and continue cooking for a further minute. Turn into another serving dish.

⑥ Serve the liver with the noodles and stir-fried vegetables as side dishes.

PREPARATION AND COOKING TIME: 20 MINUTES PLUS MARINATING

# Spicy lamb fillets
## SERVES 4

120 ml/4 fl oz/½ cup plain low-fat yoghurt
2 garlic cloves, crushed
15 ml/1 tbsp grated fresh root ginger
5 ml/1 tsp ground cumin
5 ml/1 tsp ground turmeric
30 ml/2 tbsp lemon juice
Salt and freshly ground black pepper
4 lamb fillets
Pitta bread and salad, to serve

① In a non-metallic bowl, mix together the yoghurt, garlic, ginger, cumin, turmeric and lemon juice. Season with a little salt and pepper.

② Add the lamb fillets to the marinade, turn to coat evenly and leave in a cool place for 2 hours.

③ Cook the lamb under a hot grill (broiler) for 3 minutes on each side, basting occasionally with the marinade.

④ Serve with warm pitta bread and a salad.

PREPARATION AND COOKING TIME: 15 MINUTES PLUS MARINATING

# 𝒫ork with noodles

## SERVES 4

*Marinating tenderises meat that is going to be stir-fried.
Ideally, it should be left for 1–2 hours, but even 10 minutes
will do if you are in a hurry.*

---

**450 g/1 lb pork steaks**
**30 ml/2 tbsp soy sauce**
**2 garlic cloves, crushed**
**350 g/12 oz egg noodles**
**15 ml/1 tbsp vegetable oil**
**10 ml/2 tsp sesame oil**
**1 carrot, cut into matchsticks**
**6 spring onions (scallions), sliced**
**225 g/8 oz/1 small can of water chestnuts, drained and
   halved**
**50 g/2 oz/½ cup frozen peas**

---

① Cut the pork into thin strips. Put into a bowl with 15 ml/
   1 tbsp of the soy sauce and the garlic. Stir well to ensure
   the pork is evenly coated. Cover and leave to marinate for
   10 minutes.

② Cook the noodles in plenty of boiling water for 4 minutes,
   or according to the instructions on the packet. Drain.

③ Heat the oils in a wok or large frying pan (skillet) and stir-
   fry the pork for 3–4 minutes, until browned.

④ Add the carrot, spring onions, water chestnuts and peas.
   Stir-fry for 2–3 minutes.

⑤ Add the cooked noodles and the remaining soy sauce. Stir
   well and cook until heated through.

⑥ Serve immediately.

PREPARATION AND COOKING TIME: 15 MINUTES PLUS MARINATING

# Pork steaks with apple and green pepper
## SERVES 4

15 ml/1 tbsp vegetable or sunflower oil
4 pork steaks
1 garlic clove, crushed
1 red eating (dessert) apple, cored and sliced
1 green (bell) pepper, sliced
100 g/4 oz mushrooms, sliced
150 ml/¼ pt/⅔ cup unsweetened apple juice
Salt and freshly ground black pepper
New potatoes and green vegetables, to serve

① Heat the oil in a large frying pan (skillet) and cook the pork steaks for 5 minutes on each side. Remove from the pan and keep warm.

② Put the garlic, apple, green pepper and mushrooms in the pan and cook for 1 minute.

③ Replace the pork steaks, pour in the apple juice and season to taste with a little salt and pepper. Cook uncovered for another 5–10 minutes, until the liquid has reduced and thickened slightly, and the meat is tender.

④ Serve with new potatoes and green vegetables.

PREPARATION AND COOKING TIME: 20 MINUTES

# Cassoulet

## SERVES 6

*This is an excellent family dish. It has a long cooking time,
but the preparation is easy, and once it is in the oven you
can forget about it. The breadcrumbs sprinkled on top help to
soak up excess fat. They form a delicious golden crust – but
people with diabetes should eat only a tiny bit!*

450 g/1 lb haricot beans
15 ml/1 tbsp olive or sunflower oil
100 g/4 oz streaky bacon rashers (slices), chopped
2 large onions, chopped
2 garlic cloves, crushed
450 g/1 lb pork sausages
450 ml/¾ pt/2 cups beef stock
400 g/14 oz/1 large can of tomatoes
5 ml/1 tsp dried mixed herbs
Salt and freshly ground black pepper
100 g/4 oz/2 cups fresh white breadcrumbs

① Soak the haricot beans in cold water overnight. Next day, drain the beans, put them in a pan of fresh water and cook for 1 hour.

② Preheat the oven to 160°C/325°F/gas mark 3.

③ Heat the oil in a large flameproof casserole (Dutch oven). Add the bacon and onion and fry (sauté) for 3–4 minutes. Add the garlic and pork sausages and fry for 5 minutes, turning the sausages to brown them on all sides.

④ Add the haricot beans, stock, tomatoes, and mixed herbs. Season with salt and pepper. Bring to the boil, stirring gently, then reduce the heat, cover and transfer to the oven for 1½ hours.

⑤ Remove from the oven and sprinkle the top with breadcrumbs. Bake uncovered for a further 30 minutes.

PREPARATION AND COOKING TIME: 2¾ HOURS PLUS SOAKING

# Pasta main courses

*P*asta is an ideal carbohydrate food for people with diabetes, and a popular choice for the whole family – but make sure the sauces you serve with pasta are low in fat. Use olive oil for frying (sautéing) rather than butter or margarine, and low-fat crème fraîche or plain low-fat yoghurt instead of cream. Cheese is a natural partner to pasta, but Cheddar and Parmesan cheese are both high in fat, so buy reduced-fat Cheddar and use Parmesan sparingly if at all.

I have suggested using particular pasta shapes for each of these recipes, but you can use any pasta that you have in the storecupboard – just remember to check the cooking time. Choose wholemeal pasta whenever possible (which takes slightly longer to cook), and to complete your balanced meal, serve a green salad.

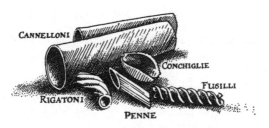

# Tagliatelle with mushroom goulash
## SERVES 4

30 ml/ 2 tbsp olive oil
1 large leek, sliced
1 green (bell) pepper, diced
450 g/1 lb button mushrooms, thickly sliced
175 g/6 oz chestnut mushrooms, halved
30 ml/2 tbsp paprika
150 ml/¼ pt/⅔ cup vegetable stock
30 ml/2 tbsp tomato purée (paste)
30 ml/2 tbsp chopped fresh parsley
Salt and freshly ground black pepper
350 g/12 oz tagliatelle
30 ml/2 tbsp low-fat crème fraîche
Sprigs of parsley, to garnish

① Heat the oil in a large frying pan (skillet) and gently cook the leek and green pepper for 2 minutes.

② Add the mushrooms and continue cooking for 5 minutes, stirring occasionally.

③ Stir in the paprika and cook for 1 minute. Add the stock, tomato purée and parsley. Season with a little salt and freshly ground pepper.

④ Cook for a further 10 minutes, stirring occasionally.

⑤ Meanwhile, cook the tagliatelli in plenty of boiling, lightly salted water for 5–7 minutes, or according to the directions on the packet.

⑥ Just before serving, stir the crème fraîche into the goulash and heat through. Serve on the drained tagliatelle, garnished with parsley sprigs.

PREPARATION AND COOKING TIME: 20 MINUTES

# *Pasta shells with sweetcorn and tuna*
## SERVES 4

---

**350 g/12 oz pasta shells**
**15 ml/1 tbsp olive oil**
**1 onion, sliced**
**1 red (bell) pepper, chopped**
**2 × 185 g/6½ oz/small cans of tuna in brine**
**400 g/14 oz/1 large can of sweetcorn (corn)**
**15 ml/1 tbsp lemon juice**
**30 ml/2 tbsp chopped fresh parsley**

---

① Cook the pasta shells in plenty of boiling, lightly salted water for about 15 minutes, or according to the instructions on the packet.

② Heat the oil in a frying pan (skillet) and gently fry (sauté) the onion and pepper until softened but not browned.

③ Drain the tuna and the sweetcorn, and add to the frying pan. Heat through gently.

④ Drain the pasta and add to the tuna mixture with the lemon juice and parsley. Heat through gently, then serve on warm plates.

PREPARATION AND COOKING TIME: 20 MINUTES

# Spaghetti Bolognese
## SERVES 4

*I have used red lentils to replace some of the meat in this Bolognese sauce. This increases the carbohydrate and fibre in the dish, and reduces the fat content.*

---

15 ml/1 tbsp olive oil
1 onion, chopped
1 garlic clove, crushed
1 celery stick, chopped
1 carrot, finely chopped
225 g/8 oz lean minced (ground) beef
100 g/4 oz/⅔ cup red lentils
100 g/4 oz mushrooms, sliced
400 g/14 oz/1 large can of tomatoes
15 ml/1 tbsp tomato purée (paste)
150 ml/¼ pt/⅔ cup beef stock
5 ml/1 tsp chopped fresh basil or oregano, or 2.5 ml/
  ½ tsp dried mixed herbs
Salt and freshly ground black pepper
350 g/12 oz spaghetti
Grated Parmesan cheese, to serve

---

① Heat the oil in a large saucepan and add the onion, garlic, celery and carrot. Fry (sauté) gently for 5 minutes.

② Add the beef and fry for a further 5 minutes, stirring continuously.

③ Add the lentils, mushrooms, tomatoes, tomato purée, stock and herbs. Season with a little salt and pepper. Bring to the boil, then reduce the heat, cover and simmer gently for 30 minutes.

④ Remove the lid and cook for a further 20–30 minutes, until the sauce has thickened. Stir frequently.

⑤ Meanwhile, cook the spaghetti in plenty of boiling, lightly salted water for 10–15 minutes, according to the instructions on the packet.

⑥ Drain the spaghetti and pile on to warm plates. Spoon the Bolognese sauce over.

⑦ Serve sprinkled with a little grated Parmesan cheese.

PREPARATION AND COOKING TIME: 1–1¼ HOURS

## *Linguine with prosciutto in a creamy sauce*
### SERVES 4

---

**350 g/12 oz linguine**
**15 ml/1 tbsp olive oil**
**6 spring onions (scallions), sliced**
**2 garlic cloves, crushed**
**3 eggs**
**150 ml/¼ pt/⅔ cup low-fat crème fraîche**
**30 ml/2 tbsp grated Parmesan cheese**
**Salt and freshly ground black pepper**
**100 g/4 oz prosciutto, cut into strips**

---

① Cook the linguine in plenty of boiling, lightly salted water for 10–12 minutes, or according to the packet instructions.

② Heat the oil in a small pan and gently fry (sauté) the onion and garlic for 3–4 minutes, until softened.

③ In a small bowl, beat together the eggs, crème fraîche and Parmesan. Season with a little salt and pepper.

④ Drain the linguine into a sieve (strainer) and then return it to the pan. Do not put it on the heat.

⑤ Immediately add the beaten egg mixture, cooked onions and garlic and the prosciutto. Toss thoroughly and serve.

PREPARATION AND COOKING TIME: 15 MINUTES

# *Tagliatelle with bacon and pesto*
### SERVES 4

15 ml/1 tbsp olive oil
2 garlic cloves, crushed
225 g/8 oz lean bacon rashers (slices), cut into strips
350 g/12 oz tagliatelle
200 ml/7 fl oz/scant 1 cup low-fat crème fraîche
45 ml/3 tbsp green pesto
Salt and freshly ground black pepper
Black olives, to garnish

① Heat the oil in a large frying pan (skillet), add the garlic and bacon and cook over a medium heat for about 5 minutes, or until the bacon is crisp and browned.

② Meanwhile, cook the tagliatelle in plenty of boiling, lightly salted water for 5–7 minutes, or according to the instructions on the packet.

③ Drain the pasta, add to the bacon mixture, and stir in the crème fraîche and pesto. Season with a little salt and black pepper.

④ Heat through for 2 minutes, then spoon on to warmed plates. Serve garnished with black olives.

PREPARATION AND COOKING TIME: 15 MINUTES

# Conchiglie with ham and mushrooms
## SERVES 4

350 g/12 oz conchiglie
30 ml/2 tbsp olive oil
175 g/6 oz mushrooms
2 garlic cloves, crushed
175 g/6 oz smoked ham, cut into strips
60 ml/4 tbsp white wine
5 ml/1 tsp chopped fresh oregano
Freshly ground black pepper

① Cook the conchiglie in plenty of boiling, lightly salted water for 10 minutes, or according to the instructions on the packet. Drain and set aside.

② Meanwhile, heat the oil in a saucepan and gently fry (sauté) the mushrooms and garlic for 5 minutes.

③ Add the smoked ham and wine and continue cooking for another 5 minutes.

④ Stir in the cooked pasta and oregano. Season well with black pepper.

PREPARATION AND COOKING TIME: 15 MINUTES

# Pasta with paprika chicken
SERVES 4

15 ml/1 tbsp sunflower or vegetable oil
4 boneless chicken breasts, skinned
1 small onion, finely chopped
5 ml/1 tsp fennel seeds
2.5 ml/½ tsp paprika
25 g/1 oz/¼ cup wholemeal flour
200 ml/7 fl oz/scant 1 cup skimmed or semi-skimmed
  milk
Salt and freshly ground black pepper
350 g/12 oz pasta

① Heat the oil in a heavy-based pan.

② Cut the chicken breasts into 1 cm/½ in cubes and put into the pan with the onion and fennel seeds. Stir-fry for 2–3 minutes until the chicken has turned white on all sides.

③ Stir in the paprika and flour and continue cooking for another minute.

④ Add the milk and stir until the sauce thickens. Reduce the heat, cover, and simmer for 10 minutes. Adjust the seasoning to taste, if necessary.

⑤ Meanwhile, cook the pasta in plenty of boiling, lightly salted water for 10–12 minutes, or according to the packet instructions. Drain well.

⑥ Spoon the pasta and paprika chicken on to warmed plates and serve hot.

PREPARATION AND COOKING TIME: 20 MINUTES

# Fusilli and spinach bake
## SERVES 4

350 g/12 oz spinach
350 g/12 oz fusilli
30 ml/2 tbsp olive oil
2 garlic cloves, crushed
50 g/2 oz/¼ cup sunflower margarine or low-fat spread
50 g/2 oz/½ cup plain (all-purpose) flour
450 ml/¾ pt/2 cups semi-skimmed milk
2.5 ml/½ tsp grated nutmeg
Salt and freshly ground black pepper
5 large tomatoes, sliced
50 g/2 oz/½ cup reduced-fat Cheddar cheese, grated

① Preheat the oven to 180°C/350°F/gas mark 4.

② Wash the spinach thoroughly. Cover the bottom of a large saucepan with a little water, add the spinach and cook for about 5 minutes, until the spinach is soft and wilted. Set aside to cool.

③ Meanwhile, cook the fusilli in plenty of boiling, lightly salted water for 10–15 minutes, or according to the packet instructions. Drain well and toss with the olive oil and garlic.

④ Melt the margarine or spread in a small, heavy-bottomed saucepan. Gradually stir in the flour, then add the milk slowly, stirring all the time until the sauce thickens. Simmer over a very low heat for 5 minutes.

⑤ Press all the liquid out of the cooked spinach and mix into the sauce with the nutmeg. Season with a little salt and pepper. Spread over the bottom of a large baking dish.

⑥ Spread the pasta over the spinach layer. Arrange the tomato slices on top and sprinkle with the grated cheese.

⑦ Bake in the preheated oven for 40–45 minutes, until the top is nicely browned.

PREPARATION AND COOKING TIME: 1–1¼ HOURS

# Seafood pasta
## SERVES 4

15 ml/1 tbsp olive oil
2 garlic cloves, sliced
1 onion, sliced
540 g/1 lb 3 oz/1 very large can of tomatoes
15 ml/1 tbsp tomato purée (paste)
150 ml/¼ pt/⅔ cup dry white wine
5 ml/1 tsp chopped fresh oregano
5 ml/1 tsp chopped fresh basil
Salt and fresh ground black pepper
350 g/12 oz tagliatelle
175 g/6 oz cooked peeled prawns (shrimp)
100 g/4 oz cooked shelled mussels
15 ml/1 tbsp chopped fresh parsley

① Heat the oil in a frying pan (skillet), add the garlic and onion and cook gently for 5 minutes, until soft.

② Add the tomatoes, tomato purée, wine and herbs. Season with a little salt and pepper. Bring to the boil and cook, uncovered, for 20–25 minutes, until thickened.

③ Meanwhile, cook the tagliatelli in plenty of boiling, lightly salted water for 5–7 minutes, or according to the instructions on the packet.

④ Add the prawns and mussels to the sauce and cook gently for 5 minutes.

⑤ Drain the pasta and arrange on a warmed serving dish. Spoon over the sauce and sprinkle with parsley.

PREPARATION AND COOKING TIME: 35 MINUTES

# Salmon and parsley pasta

SERVES 4

350 g/12 oz fusilli
450 g/1 lb salmon fillet
175 g/6 oz cherry tomatoes, halved
150 ml/¼ pt/⅔ cup low-fat crème fraîche
45 ml/3 tbsp chopped fresh parsley
Salt and freshly ground black pepper
15 ml/1 tbsp lemon juice

① Cook the fusilli in plenty of boiling, lightly salted water for 10–12 minutes.

② Meanwhile, remove the skin from the salmon and cut into bite-sized pieces. Put into a saucepan and cover with cold water. Bring to the boil, then lower the heat and simmer for 6–7 minutes, until cooked.

③ Drain the pasta and toss with the tomatoes and salmon.

④ Mix together the crème fraîche and parsley and stir into the pasta. Season with a little salt and pepper, and stir in the lemon juice.

PREPARATION AND COOKING TIME: 15 MINUTES

# Golden pasta bake
## SERVES 4

*The egg topping on this colourful pasta dish rises up to make a fluffy, golden crust.*

---

350 g/12 oz penne
175 g/6 oz broccoli florets
50 g/2 oz/¼ cup sunflower margarine or low-fat spread
225 g/8 oz shallots, quartered
2 garlic cloves, crushed
1 red (bell) pepper, sliced
50 g/2 oz/½ cup plain (all-purpose) flour
600 ml/1 pt/2½ cups skimmed milk
150 ml/¼ pt/⅔ cup dry white wine
5 ml/1 tsp Dijon mustard
Salt and freshly ground black pepper
25 g/1 oz/¼ cup reduced-fat Cheddar cheese
185 g/6¾ oz/1 small can of tuna, drained
175 g/6 oz thawed frozen sweetcorn (corn)
100 ml/3½ oz/½ cup low-fat crème fraîche
*For the topping:*
2 eggs, beaten
100 ml/3½ fl oz/scant ½ cup low-fat crème fraîche
50 g/2 oz/½ cup reduced-fat Cheddar cheese, grated

---

① Preheat the oven to 190°C/375°F/gas mark 5.

② Cook the penne in plenty of boiling, lightly salted water for 10–12 minutes, or according to the instructions on the packet. Drain.

③ Cook the broccoli in boiling, lightly salted water for 4–5 minutes, until tender but still with some 'bite'.

④ Meanwhile, melt the margarine or spread in a large pan and cook the shallots, garlic and red pepper for about 5 minutes, until softened.

⑤ Stir in the flour, cook for 1 minute, then gradually add the milk. Bring to the boil, stirring continuously until thickened. Stir in the cooked pasta, broccoli and remaining ingredients. Turn into a large, ovenproof dish.

⑦ Beat the eggs and crème fraîche together and spoon over the pasta mixture. Sprinkle with the grated cheese.

⑧ Bake in the preheated oven for 30–40 minutes, until golden brown.

PREPARATION AND COOKING TIME: 50 MINUTES

## *Pasta with fresh vegetables*
### SERVES 4

**350 g/12 oz pasta**
**15 ml/1 tbsp olive oil**
**1 onion, sliced**
**1 garlic clove, crushed**
**2 courgettes (zucchini), sliced**
**1 green (bell) pepper, sliced**
**1 red pepper, sliced**
**100 g/4 oz broccoli florets**
**Grated Parmesan cheese (optional)**

① Cook the pasta in plenty of boiling, light salted water for 10–12 minutes, or according to the packet instructions.

② Heat the oil in a frying pan (skillet). Add the onion and garlic and cook gently for 3–4 minutes until softened.

③ Add the courgettes, peppers and broccoli. Stir-fry for 4–5 minutes, until softened a little but still crisp.

④ Drain the pasta and combine with the vegetables

⑤ Sprinkle with Parmesan cheese, if using, and serve hot.

PREPARATION AND COOKING TIME: 15 MINUTES

# Vegetarian main courses

*P*ulses and grains contain plenty of fibre, so they are excellent diabetic foods and make up a perfect, well-balanced meal when served with a salad and some wholemeal bread. The following recipes can be enjoyed by anyone with or without diabetes, whether they are a vegetarian or not. More vegetarian dishes can be found in the chapters on Soups (see page 33) and Salads (see page 42).

# Tunisian aubergine with bulghar
## SERVES 4

2 aubergines (eggplants)
Salt
225 g/8 oz/2 cups bulghar (cracked wheat)
60 ml/4 tbsp olive oil
2 onions, sliced
15 ml/1 tbsp ground coriander (cilantro)
15 ml/1 tbsp ground cumin
100 g/4 oz/⅔ cup flaked (slivered) almonds
100 g/4 oz/⅔ cup raisins
Salt and freshly ground black pepper
Chopped fresh coriander or parsley, to garnish

① Cut the aubergines into 2.5 cm/1 in cubes. Put into a colander and sprinkle with salt. Leave to drain for 20 minutes, then rinse and pat dry with kitchen paper (paper towels).

② Put the bulghar in a bowl, cover with boiling water and set aside for 15–20 minutes, until all the water has absorbed and the bulghar is soft. Drain off any surplus liquid.

③ Meanwhile, heat half the oil in a large pan and fry (sauté) the onions over a moderate heat for 3–4 minutes, until soft, but not browned.

④ Add the aubergine and fry until browned all over, stirring frequently. Add the rest of the oil if it looks too dry.

⑤ Add the spices to the pan and cook for 1 minute, stirring continuously.

⑥ Lower the heat and add the almonds and raisins. Stir in the bulghar and season with a little salt and pepper.

⑦ Serve garnished with chopped coriander or parsley.

PREPARATION AND COOKING TIME: 20 MINUTES

# Lentil and vegetable hot-pot
## SERVES 4

225 g/8 oz/1⅓ cups green lentils
25 g/1 oz/¼ cup sunflower margarine or low-fat spread
1 onion, chopped
1 garlic clove, crushed (optional)
2.5 ml/½ tsp curry powder
3 celery sticks, chopped
3 carrots, sliced
15 ml/1 tbsp plain (all-purpose) flour
400 ml/14 fl oz/1¾ cups vegetable stock
Salt and freshly ground black pepper
175 g/6 oz French (green) beans
2 courgettes (zucchini), sliced
25 g/1 oz/½ cup fresh white breadcrumbs
75 g/3 oz/⅓ cup reduced-fat Cheddar cheese, grated

① Rinse and drain the lentils. Put into a saucepan with plenty of fresh, cold water, bring to the boil and boil rapidly for 10 minutes. Lower the heat and simmer for a further 20 minutes, or until tender.

② Meanwhile, melt the margarine or spread in a large saucepan and fry (sauté) the onion and garlic, if using, for about 5 minutes until softened but not browned. Add the curry powder, celery and carrots. Cover and cook gently for 5 minutes.

③ Stir in the flour, then the vegetable stock. Bring to the boil, stirring all the time. Season with a little salt and pepper and simmer for 5 minutes.

④ Add the French beans and simmer for a further 5 minutes, then add the courgettes. Continue cooking for about 10 minutes, until the vegetables are tender.

⑤ Drain the lentils and add to the vegetables. Heat through for 2–3 minutes. Taste and adjust the seasoning, then turn into a flameproof dish.

⑥ Mix the breadcrumbs and cheese together and sprinkle on top. Cook under a hot grill (broiler) until crisp and golden.

PREPARATION AND COOKING TIME: 35–40 MINUTES

# Lentil and tomato bake
## SERVES 4–6

700 g/1½ lb potatoes, peeled
30 ml/2 tbsp vegetable or sunflower oil
350 g/12 oz/2 cups split red lentils
1 large onion, chopped
30 ml/2 tbsp tomato purée (paste)
3 tomatoes, sliced
150 ml/¼ pt/⅔ cup plain low-fat yoghurt
50 g/2 oz/½ cup reduced-fat Cheddar cheese, grated

① Preheat the oven to 200°C/400°F/gas mark 6.

② Put the potatoes into a large pan of boiling, lightly salted water and cook for 20 minutes, or until soft. Drain well and slice.

③ Heat the oil in another pan, add the lentils and onion and fry (sauté) for 5 minutes. Add water to cover, bring to the boil, then reduce the heat and simmer for about 15 minutes, until all the liquid is absorbed.

④ Add the tomato purée to the lentil mixture and mix well. Spoon half the mixture into a ovenproof dish. Cover with sliced tomatoes, then add the remaining lentil mixture.

⑤ Arrange the cooked, sliced potatoes on top of the lentils. Pour over the yoghurt and sprinkle the cheese on top.

⑥ Bake in the preheated oven for 30–40 minutes, until the top is brown and bubbling.

PREPARATION AND COOKING TIME: 1 HOUR

# Lentil moussaka
## SERVES 4–6

100 g/4 oz/⅔ cup green lentils
2 aubergines (eggplants)
Salt
700 g/1½ lb potatoes
45 ml/3 tbsp olive oil
2 onions, chopped
5 ml/1 tsp dried mixed herbs
7.5 ml/1½ tsp grated nutmeg
400 g/14 oz/1 large can of tomatoes
15 ml/1 tbsp tomato purée (paste)
25 g/1 oz/2 tbsp sunflower margarine or low-fat spread
25 g/1 oz/½ cup plain (all-purpose) flour
300 ml/½ pt/1¼ cups skimmed milk
1 small egg

① Rinse and drain the lentils. Put into a saucepan with plenty of fresh, cold water, bring to the boil and boil rapidly for 10 minutes. Lower the heat and simmer for a further 20 minutes, or until tender.

② Slice the aubergines and put into a colander. Sprinkle with salt and leave to drain for 20 minutes. Rinse and pat dry with kitchen paper (paper towels).

③ Meanwhile, put the potatoes into a large pan of boiling, lightly salted water and cook for 20 minutes, or until soft. Drain and slice.

④ Preheat the oven to 190°C/375°F/gas mark 5.

⑤ Heat 30 ml/2 tbsp of the olive oil in a frying pan (skillet) and fry (sauté) the aubergine slices until golden brown. Remove with a slotted spoon and set aside.

⑥ Add the remaining olive oil to the pan and fry the onions until they are soft. Then add the cooked lentils, herbs, 5 ml/1 tsp of the nutmeg, the tomatoes and tomato purée. Bring to the boil, reduce the heat and simmer for 5 minutes.

⑦ Arrange a layer of aubergine in the bottom of a large, ovenproof dish. Follow this with a layer of cooked potato and a layer of lentil mixture. Repeat until all the ingredients are used up, ending with a layer of aubergine slices.

⑧ To make the sauce, melt the margarine or spread in a saucepan, stir in the flour, then gradually add the milk. Bring to the boil, stirring all the time, then reduce the heat and simmer for 2–3 minutes, until the sauce has thickened. Remove the pan from the heat, add the remaining nutmeg, and allow to cool slightly before beating in the egg.

⑨ Pour the sauce over the moussaka and bake in the preheated oven for 45 minutes.

PREPARATION AND COOKING TIME: 1½ HOURS

# *Winter vegetable casserole*
## SERVES 4–6

15 ml/1 tbsp olive oil
1 onion, sliced
2 garlic cloves, crushed
5 ml/1 tsp chilli powder
2.5 ml/½ tsp made English mustard
30 ml/2 tbsp wine vinegar
15 ml/1 tbsp tomato purée (paste)
400 g/14 oz/1 large can of chopped tomatoes
300 ml/½ pt/1¼ cups vegetable stock
Salt and freshly ground black pepper
1 small swede (rutabaga), diced
350 g/12 oz carrots, sliced
350 g/12 oz parsnips, sliced
100 g/4 oz button mushrooms, sliced
425 g/15 oz/1 large can of chick peas (garbanzos),
  drained and rinsed
425 g/15 oz/1 large can of borlotti beans, drained and
  rinsed
60 ml/4 tbsp chopped fresh parsley

① Heat the oil in a large pan. Fry (sauté) the onion and garlic over a low heat for 3–4 minutes, until softened and translucent but not browned.

② Add the chilli powder, mustard and vinegar and continue cooking for 1 minute.

③ Stir in the tomato purée, tomatoes and stock. Season with a little salt and pepper. Add the swede, carrots and parsnips and simmer for 20 minutes, or until the vegetables are tender.

④ Add the mushrooms, chick peas and beans, and heat through for a further 5 minutes.

⑤ Sprinkle with chopped parsley before serving.

PREPARATION AND COOKING TIME: 30 MINUTES

# Bean goulash
SERVES 4

30 ml/2 tbsp sunflower or vegetable oil
2 onions, sliced
2 garlic cloves, crushed
15 ml/1 tbsp paprika
425 g/15 oz/large can of red kidney beans
425 g/15 oz/large can of borlotti or butter (lima) beans
400 g/14 oz/large can of tomatoes
Salt and freshly ground black pepper
Pitta bread, to serve

① Heat the oil in a saucepan and fry (sauté) the onion and garlic for 3–4 minutes.

② Add the paprika and cook for another minute.

③ Rinse and drain the kidney beans and add to the pan with the tomatoes.

④ Simmer gently for 5 minutes until all the ingredients are heated through.

⑤ Season to taste with a little salt and pepper.

⑥ Serve with warm pitta bread.

PREPARATION AND COOKING TIME: 10 MINUTES

# Stuffed peppers with tomato sauce
## SERVES 4

450 g/1 lb tomatoes, peeled and chopped
30 ml/2 tbsp olive oil
2 onions, finely chopped
Salt and freshly ground black pepper
150 ml/¼ pt/⅔ cup vegetable stock
5 ml/1 tsp chopped fresh thyme
4 large red or green (bell) peppers
2 garlic cloves, crushed
175 g/6 oz/1½ cups cooked brown or basmati rice
25 g/1 oz/¼ cup frozen peas, defrosted
25 g/1 oz/¼ cup thawed frozen sweetcorn (corn)
15 ml/1 tbsp chopped fresh thyme
15 ml/1 tbsp chopped fresh parsley

① First make the tomato sauce. Pierce the skins of the tomatoes and put them in boiling water for a few minutes until they start to peel. Remove the skins and chop.

② Heat 15 ml/1 tbsp of the oil in a pan and cook half the chopped onion for 3–4 minutes until softened. Add the tomatoes, season with a little salt and pepper, and cook gently for 25 minutes. Add the stock and thyme and continue cooking for another 5 minutes.

③ Meanwhile, cut the tops off the peppers and remove the core and seeds. Blanch the peppers in boiling water for 2 minutes. Plunge into cold water, drain, and leave to cool.

④ Preheat the oven to 190°C/375°F/gas mark 5.

⑤ Heat the remaining oil in a frying pan, add the remaining onion and the garlic and cook gently for 3–4 minutes, until softened. Add the cooked rice, peas, sweetcorn and herbs, and season with a little salt and pepper. Heat gently for a further 3–4 minutes, stirring constantly.

⑥ Arrange the peppers in an ovenproof dish and spoon the rice mixture into them. Top each with 15 ml/1 tbsp of the tomato sauce.

⑦ Pour about 1 cm/½ warm water into the dish around the peppers. Bake in the preheated oven for about 40 minutes, until the peppers are tender.

⑧ To serve, reheat the remaining tomato sauce and pour over the peppers.

PREPARATION AND COOKING TIME: 1 HOUR 20 MINUTES

# Quick chilli beans
### SERVES 4

2 × 425 g/15 oz/large cans of red kidney beans
30 ml/2 tbsp sunflower or vegetable oil
2 onions, sliced
1 green (bell) pepper, sliced
1 red pepper, sliced
5 ml/1 tsp chilli powder
5 ml/1 tsp dried mixed herbs
15 ml/1 tbsp tomato purée (paste)
Brown rice or pitta bread, to serve

① Drain the beans into a sieve (strainer) and rinse thoroughly under cold, running water.

② Heat the oil in a saucepan and gently fry (sauté) the onions and peppers for 5 minutes.

③ Add the beans and the rest of the ingredients and cook for another 10 minutes.

④ Serve with brown rice or warm pitta bread.

PREPARATION AND COOKING TIME: 15 MINUTES

# Oriental rice
## SERVES 4

*This versatile dish can be served hot as a main meal, or cold as part of a buffet.*

---

275 g/10 oz/1¼ cups brown rice
15 ml/1 tbsp sunflower or vegetable oil
1 red (bell) pepper, diced
1 onion, sliced
225 g/8 oz beansprouts
50 g/2 oz/⅓ cup raisins
150 ml/¼ pt/⅔ cup unsweetened pineapple juice
75 g/3 oz/¾ cup canned or thawed frozen sweetcorn (corn)
5 ml/1 tsp soy sauce
50 g/2 oz/½ cup flaked (slivered) almonds, toasted
15 ml/1 tbsp chopped fresh parsley or coriander (cilantro)

---

① Cook the rice in plenty of boiling, lightly salted water for 30–35 minutes. Drain and rinse well.

② Meanwhile, heat the oil in a large frying pan (skillet). Add the pepper and onion and stir-fry for 3–4 minutes.

③ Add the beansprouts and continue stir-frying for another 2–3 minutes.

④ Add the raisins, pineapple juice, sweetcorn and soy sauce. Simmer for 5 minutes, then remove from the heat.

⑤ Add the cooked rice and stir to combine all the ingredients.

⑥ Sprinkle over the almonds and chopped parsley or coriander.

PREPARATION AND COOKING TIME: 40 MINUTES

# Spiced couscous with courgettes
### SERVES 4

5 ml/1 tsp cumin seeds
4 cloves
500 ml/17 fl oz/2¼ cups vegetable stock
6 cardamom pods, lightly crushed
1 cinnamon stick
2 bay leaves
300 g/11 oz/2¾ cups couscous
2–3 courgettes (zucchini), sliced
30–45 ml/2–3 tbsp olive oil
Salt and freshly ground black pepper
15 ml/1 tbsp chopped fresh parsley
30 ml/2 tbsp pine nuts, toasted

①  Lightly toast the cumin seeds and cloves in a dry saucepan for 1–2 minutes.

②  Add the stock, cardamom pods, cinnamon and bay leaves. Bring to the boil and simmer for 2 minutes.

③  Remove the pan from the heat and add the couscous. Stir well, cover the pan and leave for about 5 minutes, until the stock has been absorbed.

④  Meanwhile, heat 15 ml/1 tbsp of oil in a frying pan (skillet) and add a single layer of courgette slices. Cook for about 2 minutes, then turn and cook the other side until they are golden brown. Transfer to a warm plate and cook the remaining courgette slices in the same way, adding more oil as necessary. Season the cooked courgettes with a little salt and pepper and sprinkle with chopped parsley.

⑤  Remove the cinnamon stick and bay leaves from the couscous and season lightly. Sprinkle with the toasted pine nuts.

⑥  Serve the hot couscous with the courgettes as a side dish.

PREPARATION AND COOKING TIME: 15 MINUTES

# Spicy aubergines with brown rice
### SERVES 4

350 g/12 oz/1½ cups brown rice
3 aubergines (eggplants)
Salt
45–60 ml/3–4 tbsp olive oil
2 onions, sliced
2 garlic cloves, crushed
1.5 ml/¼ tsp cayenne
1.5 ml/¼ tsp ground cloves
5 ml/1 tsp ground cumin
5 ml/1 tsp ground coriander (cilantro)
450 g/1 lb tomatoes
15 ml/1 tbsp chopped fresh mint
50 g/2 oz/⅓ cup raisins
Freshly ground black pepper
Chopped fresh parsley, to garnish

① Cook the rice in plenty of boiling, lightly salted water for 40–45 minutes, until tender. Drain.

② Cut the aubergines into 2.5 cm/1 in cubes. Put into a colander, sprinkle with salt and leave for 20 minutes to drain. Rinse and pat dry with kitchen paper (paper towels).

③ Heat the oil in a large frying pan (skillet). Add the onions and garlic and fry (sauté) for 3–4 minutes, until softened. Stir in the cayenne and spices and cook for a further 2 minutes.

④ Add the aubergine cubes and brown on all sides.

⑤ Stir in the tomatoes, mint, raisins and plenty of pepper. Cook gently until almost all the liquid has evaporated and the aubergines are tender.

⑥ To serve, spoon over the cooked rice and garnish with chopped parsley.

PREPARATION AND COOKING TIME: 45 MINUTES

# Polenta and mushroom bake

## SERVES 4

350 g/12 oz/3 cups polenta
Salt and freshly ground black pepper
30 ml/2 tbsp olive oil
350 g/12 oz mushrooms, sliced
50 g/2 oz/¼ cup sunflower margarine or low-fat spread
50 g/2 oz/½ cup plain (all-purpose) flour
450 ml/¾ pt/2 cups semi-skimmed milk
25 g/1 oz/¼ cup Parmesan cheese, grated

1. Preheat the oven to 200°C/400°F/gas mark 6.

2. In a saucepan, blend the polenta with four times its volume of water. Bring to the boil and simmer for 3–4 minutes, stirring continuously. Add a pinch of salt. Remove from the heat and allow to stand for 2 minutes.

3. Heat the olive oil in a frying pan (skillet), add the mushrooms and cook for 3–4 minutes, stirring frequently.

4. Melt the margarine or spread in a heavy-bottomed saucepan. Gradually stir in the flour, then add the milk slowly, stirring continuously until the sauce thickens. Season to taste with a little salt and pepper and simmer over a very low heat for 4–5 minutes.

5. Slice the cooled polenta in half and place one half in an ovenproof dish. Spread half the mushrooms on top and cover with half the sauce. Repeat the layers and sprinkle over the Parmesan cheese.

6. Bake in the preheated oven for 25–30 minutes, until the top is sizzling and golden brown.

7. Serve cut into portions.

PREPARATION AND COOKING TIME: 45 MINUTES

# Vegetable lasagne
## SERVES 4

---

450 g/1 lb spinach
15 ml/1 tbsp olive oil
1 onion, sliced
2 garlic cloves, crushed
1 green (bell) pepper, chopped
2–3 courgettes (zucchini), sliced
400 g/14 oz/1 large can of chopped tomatoes
30 ml/2 tbsp chopped fresh basil
Salt and freshly ground black pepper
225 g/8 oz no-need-to-precook lasagne
40 g/1½ oz/3 tbsp sunflower margarine or low-fat spread
50 g/2 oz/½ cup reduced-fat Cheddar cheese, grated
30 ml/2 tbsp plain (all-purpose) flour
300 ml/½ pt/1¼ cups semi-skimmed milk

---

① Preheat the oven to 180°C/350°F/gas mark 4.

② Wash the spinach thoroughly. Cover the bottom of a large saucepan with a little water, add the spinach and cook for about 5 minutes, until the spinach is soft and wilted. Drain and squeeze out all the liquid.

③ Heat the oil in a frying pan (skillet) and gently cook the onion and garlic for 2–3 minutes. Add the pepper and courgettes and cook for another 5 minutes.

④ Stir in the tomatoes and basil. Season with a little salt and black pepper.

⑤ Melt the margarine or spread in a small pan, stir in the flour and cook for 1 minute. Gradually stir in the milk and bring to the boil, stirring continuously, until the sauce has thickened. Stir in half the Cheddar cheese.

⑥ Spoon half the vegetable mixture into a large, flat, ovenproof dish, then add half the spinach and half the lasagne. Spoon over half the sauce. Repeat the layers and sprinkle over the remaining cheese.

⑦ Bake in the preheated oven for 35–40 minutes, until the top is browned and bubbling.

PREPARATION AND COOKING TIME: 1 HOUR

# Egg fried rice
### SERVES 2

*If you have some rice and vegetables left from a previous meal, this is a good way of using them up to make a quick, nutritious lunch dish.*

**3 eggs**
**Salt and freshly ground black pepper**
**15–30 ml/1–2 tbsp sunflower or vegetable oil**
**1 small onion, chopped**
**50 g/2 oz button mushrooms, sliced**
**50 g/2 oz/½ cup canned or cooked frozen peas**
**50 g/2 oz/½ cup canned or cooked frozen sweetcorn (corn)**
**175 g/6 oz/1½ cups cooked brown or basmati rice**
**15 ml/1 tbsp soy sauce**

① Beat the eggs in a bowl and season with a little salt and black pepper.

② Heat half the oil in a frying pan (skillet) and pour in the beaten egg. Cook for 2–3 minutes until the underside is set, then turn over and cook the other side. Remove to a warmed plate and keep warm.

③ Heat the remaining oil in the frying pan, add the onion and mushrooms and cook gently over a low heat for 3–4 minutes, until softened.

④ Add the peas, sweetcorn and rice and stir-fry for another 3–4 minutes, until heated through. Add the soy sauce.

⑤ To serve, cut the egg into strips and arrange on top of the rice mixture.

PREPARATION AND COOKING TIME: 15 MINUTES

# *Basmati and cashew nut pilaff*
### SERVES 4

---

350 g/12 oz basmati rice
15 ml/1 tbsp sunflower or vegetable oil
1 onion, sliced
1 garlic clove, crushed
1 large carrot, grated
5 ml/1 tsp cumin seeds
10 ml/2 tsp ground coriander
4 cardamom pods, crushed
600 ml/1 pt/2½ cups vegetable stock
1 bay leaf
Salt and freshly ground black pepper
75 g/3 oz/¾ cup unsalted cashew nuts
15 ml/1 tbsp chopped fresh coriander (cilantro)

---

① Wash the rice thoroughly under cold, running water. Drain well.

② Heat the oil in a large frying pan (skillet) and gently fry (sauté) the onion, garlic and carrot over a low heat for 4–5 minutes, until softened.

③ Stir in the rice and spices and stir-fry for 2 minutes.

④ Add the stock and bay leaf, and season with a little salt and pepper. Bring to the boil, cover, reduce the heat and simmer gently for about 10 minutes, until the rice is cooked and all the liquid has been used up.

⑤ Stir in the nuts and scatter the coriander over the top.

PREPARATION AND COOKING TIME: 20 MINUTES

# Spicy chick peas with tomato
## SERVES 4

2 × 425 g/15 oz/large cans of chick peas (garbanzos)
30 ml/2 tbsp sunflower or vegetable oil
2 onions, sliced
2 garlic cloves, crushed
5 ml/1 tsp ground turmeric
5 ml/1 tsp paprika
5 ml/1 tsp ground cumin
5 ml/1 tsp ground coriander
5 ml/1 tsp garam masala
400 g/14 oz/1 large can of tomatoes
Salt and freshly ground black pepper
Brown rice or naan bread, to serve

① Drain the chick peas through a sieve (strainer).

② Heat the oil in a saucepan and fry (sauté) the onions and garlic for about 5 minutes, until soft.

③ Add all the spices and continue cooking for another 2 minutes, stirring all the time.

④ Add the tomatoes and continue cooking until they are soft.

⑤ Add the chick peas, stir well, and cook for another 5 minutes. Season with salt and pepper.

⑥ Serve with brown rice or naan bread.

PREPARATION AND COOKING TIME: 20 MINUTES

# Desserts

*D*esserts are not completely forbidden to diabetics, as some people seem to think. A little sugar occasionally should not upset blood-sugar levels. To be on the safe side, sweeten your dessert recipes a little at a time, just to taste. Many of the recipes given here are naturally sweetened with apple juice, fresh or dried fruits, or sometimes a little honey. Low-fat yoghurt or fromage frais can be enjoyed on their own, or with a fruit dessert, but I would suggest that you avoid cream, as it is high in fat, except for a special treat.

When you have been on a healthy diet for a couple of months, you may find that you lose your taste for sweet things.

# Rice pudding with raisins
## SERVES 4

*The raisins, which are added towards the end of cooking time, add natural sweetness to this rice pudding. You can use sultanas (golden raisins) or chopped, stoned (pitted) dates instead of raisins, if you prefer.*

100 g/4 oz/½ cup round-grain pudding rice
900 ml/1½ pts/3¾ cups skimmed or semi-skimmed milk
25 g/1 oz/2 tbsp sunflower margarine or low-fat spread
A pinch of grated nutmeg
2 thinly pared twists of lemon rind
75 g/3 oz/½ cup raisins

① Wash the rice thoroughly under cold, running water.

② Put the washed rice into a saucepan with the milk, margarine or spread, nutmeg and lemon rind. Bring to the boil, reduce the heat, cover and simmer gently for 45 minutes. Remove the lemon peel, add the raisins and continue cooking for a further 10 minutes.

③ Spoon the rice pudding into a flameproof serving dish and put under a hot grill (broiler) until the top is browned.

④ Serve warm.

PREPARATION AND COOKING TIME: 1 HOUR

# Apricot and apple pudding
### SERVES 6–8

175 g/6 oz/1 cup dried apricots
2 eating (dessert) apples, sliced
300 ml/½ pt/1¼ cups water
100 g/4 oz/1 cup porridge oats
100 g/4 oz/1 cup wholemeal flour
50 g/2 oz/⅓ cup raisins
50 g/2 oz/½ cup almonds, finely chopped
10 ml/2 tsp ground cinnamon
25 g/1 oz/¼ cup sesame seeds
100 g/4 oz/½ cup sunflower margarine or low-fat spread
45 ml/3 tbsp concentrated apple juice
Plain low-fat yoghurt or crème fraîche, to serve (optional)

① Put the apricots into a bowl, cover with cold water and leave to soak overnight.

② Put the apricots and apple slices into a pan with the water. Bring to the boil, then reduce the heat, cover and simmer for about 10 minutes, or until the apricots are soft. Set aside to cool slightly.

③ Preheat the oven to 180°C/350°F/gas mark 4.

④ Mix together the oats, flour, raisins, almonds, cinnamon and most of the sesame seeds, retaining 5 ml/1 tsp for sprinkling over the pudding.

⑤ Melt the margarine or spread in a small pan. Pour over the oat mixture. Add the apple juice and mix well. Press half the oat mixture into the base of an 18 cm/7 in round, loose-bottomed tin.

⑥ Drain any excess liquid from the apricots and apples and spoon over the oat mixture. Spread the rest of the oat mixture on top, pressing down well. Sprinkle with the reserved sesame seeds.

⑦ Bake in the oven for 30–40 minutes. Allow to stand in the tin for 5 minutes before serving with low-fat yoghurt or crème fraîche, if liked.

PREPARATION AND COOKING TIME: 50 MINUTES PLUS SOAKING

# ℙlum cobbler
## SERVES 4

450 g/1 lb plums, stones removed
2.5 ml/½ tsp grated lemon rind
10 ml/2 tsp lemon juice
15 g/½ oz/1 tbsp caster (superfine) sugar, or to taste
*For the topping:*
75 g/3 oz/¾ cup plain (all-purpose) flour
2.5 ml/½ tsp baking powder
A pinch of salt
15 g/½ oz/1 tbsp caster sugar
25 g/1 oz/2 tbsp margarine or low-fat spread
1 small egg, beaten
15 ml/1 tbsp skimmed or semi-skimmed milk

① Preheat the oven to 200°C/400°F/gas mark 6.

② Put the plums into a pudding dish with the lemon rind and juice, and sugar to taste.

③ To make the topping, sift the dry ingredients into a mixing bowl and rub in the margarine or spread until it resembles fine breadcrumbs. Fold in the beaten egg and then the milk, to make a soft dough.

④ Knead the dough lightly and divide into eight portions. Make each portion into a round, flat cake and arrange on top of the plums.

⑤ Bake in the preheated oven for 25–30 minutes, until the topping is golden brown.

PREPARATION AND COOKING TIME: 45 MINUTES

# Spiced pears
## SERVES 4

4 pears
300 ml/½ pt/1¼ cups apple juice
5 ml/1 tsp ground cinnamon
2.5 ml/½ tsp grated nutmeg
2 cloves
50 g/2 oz/½ cup bulghar (cracked wheat)
60 ml/4 tbsp plain low-fat yoghurt or fromage frais,
  to serve

① Halve the pears and remove the cores.

② Put the pears into a pan with all the other ingredients. Bring to the boil, reduce the heat and simmer gently for 10 minutes, until the pears are just soft.

③ Discard the cloves. Serve hot or cold, topped with fromage frais or yoghurt.

PREPARATION AND COOKING TIME: 10 MINUTES

# Peach and apricot compôte
## SERVES 4

450 g/1 lb small peaches
450 g/1 lb apricots
150 ml/¼ pt/⅔ cup apple juice
1 cinnamon stick
15 ml/1 tbsp clear honey
Plain low-fat yoghurt or crème fraîche, to serve

① Wash the fruit, then halve and stone (pit) them.

② Put into a pan with the apple juice, cinnamon and honey. Bring to the boil, then reduce the heat, cover and simmer gently for 10–15 minutes, until soft.

③ Leave to cool, then serve with yoghurt or crème fraîche.

PREPARATION AND COOKING TIME: 20–25 MINUTES

# Blackberry fool
## SERVES 4

*This is best made in early autumn with fresh blackberries, but you can also use frozen blackberries, or canned blackberries in natural juice.*

**350 g/12 oz blackberries**
**30 ml/2 tbsp custard powder**
**300 ml/½ pt/1¼ cups skimmed or semi-skimmed milk**
**300 ml/½ pt/1¼ cups plain low-fat yoghurt**
**Caster (superfine) sugar, to taste**

① Put the blackberries in a saucepan with about 45 ml/3 tbsp water and cook gently for 5–10 minutes until soft. Liquidise the cooked fruit or push through a sieve (strainer).

② Put the custard powder into a bowl and mix to a thin paste with a little of the milk. Heat the rest of the milk to boiling point in a small saucepan, then pour over the custard powder, stirring all the time until it thickens. If it is too thin, return the custard to the saucepan and bring to the boil again, stirring continuously until it has thickened sufficiently. Leave the custard to cool.

③ Add the puréed fruit and yoghurt to the cooled custard and mix them thoroughly together. Sweeten to taste and chill for at least 1 hour before serving.

PREPARATION TIME: 15–20 MINUTES PLUS CHILLING

# Orange mango fool
### SERVES 4

**2 ripe mangoes**
**150 ml/¼ pt/⅔ cup plain low-fat yoghurt**
**Juice and grated rind of ½ orange**

① Peel the mangoes, cut the flesh off the stones (pits) and put into a food processor or liquidiser. Add the yoghurt and orange juice and process until smooth.

② Spoon into a serving dish and sprinkle the grated orange rind on top.

PREPARATION TIME: 5 MINUTES

# Apple fool
### SERVES 4

**300 ml/½ pt/1¼ cups plain low-fat yoghurt**
**4 eating (dessert) apples, grated**
**Grated rind and juice of 1 lemon**
**Clear honey, to taste**

① Mix the yoghurt, grated apples and lemon rind and juice together. Sweeten to taste with honey.

② Spoon into four individual serving dishes and chill well before serving.

PREPARATION TIME: 5 MINUTES PLUS CHILLING

# Baked apples
## SERVES 4

4 cooking (tart) apples
50 g/2 oz/⅓ cup raisins
5 ml/1 tsp ground cinnamon
5 ml/1 tsp grated nutmeg
Plain low-fat yoghurt, fromage frais or crème fraîche,
   to serve.

① Preheat the oven to 180°C/350°F/gas mark 4.

② Core the apples and make two or three slits in the skins,
   from top to bottom Place them in an ovenproof dish.

③ Mix the raisins with the spices and fill the centre of each
   apple with the mixture.

④ Bake in the preheated oven for 30–35 minutes, until the
   apples are cooked through.

⑤ Serve hot with yoghurt, fromage frais or crème fraîche.

PREPARATION AND COOKING TIME: 40 MINUTES

# Hot fruit salad
### SERVES 4

75 g/3 oz/½ cup dried apricots
50 g/2 oz/⅓ cup prunes
50 g/2 oz/⅓ cup dried figs
50 g/2 oz/⅓ dried apple slices
300 ml/½ pt/1¼ cups apple juice
15 ml/1 tbsp brandy (optional)
Plain low-fat yoghurt, to serve

① Place the dried fruits in a bowl with the apple juice and leave to soak overnight.

② Transfer to a saucepan. Bring to the boil, then lower the heat and simmer for 15 minutes.

③ Turn into a serving bowl. Pour over the brandy, if using, and serve with yoghurt.

PREPARATION AND COOKING TIME: 15 MINUTES PLUS SOAKING

# Red plum dessert
### SERVES 4

450 g/1 lb dark red plums
10 ml/2 tsp clear honey
30 ml/2 tbsp red wine
4–6 cardamom pods
15 ml/1 tbsp brandy
Plain low-fat yoghurt, fromage frais or crème fraîche,
    to serve.

① Wash the plums and put them in a pan with the honey, wine and cardamom pods. Simmer over a low heat until the plums are just starting to disintegrate.

② Add the brandy and gently heat through again.

③ Transfer to a serving dish, and serve with yoghurt, fromage frais or crème fraîche.

PREPARATION AND COOKING TIME: 10 MINUTES

# *Real fruit jelly*
### SERVES 4–6

2 tangerines, peeled and segmented
1 green eating (dessert) apple, cored and sliced
2 kiwi fruit, sliced
A small bunch of green seedless grapes
1 packet of orange-flavoured sugar-free jelly (jello)
   crystals
Plain low-fat yoghurt, fromage frais or crème fraîche,
   to serve

① Put the prepared fruit into a serving bowl.

② Pour 225 ml/8 fl oz/1 cup of boiling water into a jug.
   Sprinkle over the jelly crystals and stir until dissolved.
   Make up to 600 ml/1 pt/2½ cups with cold water and pour
   over the fruit. Leave to cool, then put into the fridge to set.

③ Serve cold with yoghurt, fromage frais or crème fraîche.

### PREPARATION TIME: 10 MINUTES PLUS SETTING

# *Strawberry mousse*
### SERVES 4

1 packet of strawberry-flavoured sugar-free jelly (jello)
   crystals
600 ml/1 pt/2½ cups water
300 ml/½ pt/1¼ cups whipping cream, whipped
225 g/8 oz fresh or thawed frozen strawberries, chopped

① Pour 225 ml/8 fl oz/1 cup of boiling water into a jug.
   Sprinkle over the jelly crystals and stir until dissolved.
   Make up to 600 ml/1 pt/2½ cups. Leave until cool, but do
   not allow to set.

② Whip the cream. Whip the jelly and fold in the whipped
   cream. Fold in the chopped strawberries. Pour into a
   serving dish and chill until set. Serve cold.

### PREPARATION TIME: 15 MINUTES PLUS SETTING

# $\mathcal{P}$each and raspberry trifle
### SERVES 4

---

**425 g/15 oz/1 large can of peaches in natural juice**
**175 g/6 oz thawed frozen raspberries**
**1 packet of raspberry-flavoured sugar-free jelly (jello)**
  **crystals**
**30 ml/2 tbsp custard powder**
**15 g/½ oz/1 tbsp caster (superfine) sugar**
**300 ml/½ pt/1¼ cups skimmed or semi-skimmed milk**
**150 ml/¼ pt/⅔ cup whipping cream, whipped**
**15 ml/1 tbsp flaked (slivered) almonds, toasted**

---

① Drain the peaches and reserve the juice. Arrange the peaches and raspberries in the bottom of a trifle bowl.

② Pour 225 ml/8 fl oz/1 cup of boiling water into a jug. Sprinkle over the jelly crystals and stir until dissolved. Make up to 600 ml/1 pt/2½ cups using the reserved peach juice. Pour the jelly over the fruit and leave to set.

③ Put the custard powder and sugar into a bowl. Mix the powder to a thin paste with a little of the milk. Heat the rest of the milk to boiling point in a small saucepan, then pour over the custard powder, stirring all the time until it thickens. (If it doesn't thicken enough, return the custard to the saucepan and bring to the boil again, stirring continuously until it has thickened sufficiently.)

④ Pour the custard over the fruit and jelly. Top with whipped cream and toasted almonds.

⑤ Chill for at least an hour before serving cold.

PREPARATION TIME: 15 MINUTES PLUS CHILLING

# Lemon soufflé

### SERVES 4

---

1 packet of lemon-flavoured sugar-free jelly (jello)
  crystals
450 ml/¾ pt/2 cups water
Grated rind and juice of 1 lemon
150 ml/¼ pt/⅔ cup double (heavy) cream
15 ml/1 tbsp semi-skimmed milk
2 eggs, separated

---

① Put 150 ml/¼ pt/⅔ cup of water into a small saucepan over a low heat. Sprinkle over the jelly crystals and stir until dissolved. Make up to 450 ml/¾ pt/2 cups with cold water.

② Add the lemon rind and juice and leave until cool, but do not allow to set.

③ Whip the cream and milk until thick.

④ Whisk the egg whites until very stiff.

⑤ When the jelly is just beginning to set, whisk in the egg yolks, then fold in the whipped cream and egg whites.

⑥ Spoon into individual bowls and chill until set.

PREPARATION TIME: 15 MINUTES PLUS SETTING

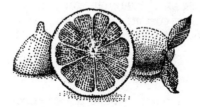

# Summer fruits cheesecake
### SERVES 8

75 g/3 oz/⅓ cup sunflower margarine or low-fat spread
175 g/6 oz digestive biscuits (graham crackers)
3 eggs, separated
300 ml/½ pt/1¼ cups semi-skimmed milk
15 g/½ oz/1 tbsp caster (superfine) sugar
15 g/½ oz/1 tbsp gelatine
30 ml/2 tbsp water
225 g/8 oz/1 cup low-fat cream cheese
Grated rind and juice of 1 lemon
450 g/1 lb summer fruits such as strawberries,
    raspberries, redcurrants

① Melt the margarine or spread in a small saucepan. Crush the biscuits (cookies) and stir into the margarine or spread. Spoon the mixture into the base of a loose-bottomed 15 cm/6 in cake tin (pan). Chill while making the filling.

② Whisk the egg yolks, then put into a saucepan with the milk and heat gently until thickened, stirring continuously. Remove from the heat and add the sugar.

③ Whisk the egg whites until stiff.

④ Put the gelatine into a small bowl and add the water. Set the bowl over a pan of simmering water until the gelatine has dissolved.

⑤ Beat the cream cheese until soft and fluffy, then whisk in the gelatine, custard, lemon rind and juice. Continue whisking until the mixture thickens.

⑥ Fold in the whisked egg whites and spoon the mixture over the biscuit base. Chill in the fridge until set.

⑦ Just before serving, remove the cheesecake from the tin and put on to a serving plate. Decorate with the fresh fruit.

PREPARATION TIME: 40 MINUTES PLUS CHILLING

# Useful addresses

## General information
Diabetes UK is a registered charity that helps people with diabetes and supports diabetes research. Members receive a copy of *Balance* magazine every two months, and have access to a telephone helpline that answers general medical, diet and welfare queries. A vast range of books, leaflets, videos and tapes covering all aspects of living with diabetes is available from Diabetes UK, in English and other languages.

Diabetes UK
Central Office
10 Queen Anne Street
London W1M 0BD
Tel: 020 7323 1531
www.diabetes.org.uk

Diabetes UK Northern Ireland
John Gibson House
257 Lisburn Road
Belfast BT9 7EN
Tel: 028 9066 6646

Diabetes UK Northern and Yorkshire
Birch House
80 Eastmount Road
Darlington DL1 1LE
Tel: 01325 488606

Diabetes UK North West
65 Bewsey Street
Warrington WA2 7JQ
Tel: 01925 653281

Diabetes UK Scotland
4th Floor, 34 West George Street
Glasgow G2 1DA
Tel: 0141 332 2700

Diabetes UK Cymru
Quebec House
Castlebridge
Cowbridge Road East
Cardiff CF11 9AB
Tel: 029 2066 8276

Diabetes UK West Midlands
1 Eldon Court
Eldon Street
Walsall WS1 2JP
Tel: 01922 614500

## Information about diet
British Dietetic Association
5th Floor, Elizabeth House
22 Suffolk Street
Queensway
Birmingham B1 1LS
Tel: 0121 616 4900

## Emergency identification system
Medic Alert Foundation
1 Bridge Wharf
156 Caledonian Road
London N1 9UU
Tel: 020 7833 3034

# further reading

Richard K Bernstein, *Dr Bernstein's Diabetes Solution: A Complete Guide to Achieving Normal Blood Sugars,* Little Brown, 1997

Robert Buckman and John Cleese, *What You Really Need to Know About Diabetes,* Marshall, 1999

Dr Stephen Colagiuri, Dr Kaye Foster-Powell and Dr Jennie Brand Miller, *The Glucose Revolution,* Hodder & Stoughton, 2000

Charles Fox, Sue Judd, Peter Sonkson, Sir Harry Secombe and Harry Keen, *Diabetes at Your Fingertips,* Class Publishing, 1998

Ragnar Hanas, *Insulin-Dependent Diabetes in Children, Adolescents and Adults – How to Become an Expert on Your Own Diabetes,* Piara Publishing, 1998

Rowan Hillson, *Diabetes: The Complete Guide,* Vermilion, 1996

Dr P H Wise, *Understanding Your Diabetes: For People with Insulin-Dependent (Type 1) Diabetes,* Foulsham, 1999

Dr P H Wise, *Understanding Your Diabetes: For People with Non-Insulin-Dependent (Type 2) Diabetes,* Foulsham, 1999

# Index